LEARNING

TO

SEE

AND OTHER SHORT STORIES AND MEMOIRS FROM SENEGAL

Man with Headdress of Memories, 23" x 16" 2008

Mask by Martin Beadle, RPCV Senegal 1966-68

GARY ENGELBERG

INTRODUCTION

◇◇

I t's early September 2015 in Senegal. We are about three quarters of the way through the rainy season. This has been one of those years that gives the impression of having passed by in overdrive. Suddenly January turned to May while I was still getting used to writing 2015 on my checks. Five days ago, September 1, marked my fifty years in Senegal...

The years too have passed quickly. When I decided to write, the short stories and memoirs in this book came quickly as well, like ripe mangos falling from the tree. They are accounts of real people and real events with some changes in names and details, as well as fictional stories with invented characters that are inspired by a composite of real events.

With its roots in the 12ᵗʰ century, and located on a cross-roads where different world cultures have met and mixed, Senegal has had the time to develop intricate mechanisms to manage diversity and bind people together in non-conflictual relationships. While its architectural achievements are modest on the world scale, its social architecture has the beauty of the Taj Mahal in its balance and perfection. These social mechanisms are reflected in the predominant cultural values of this old society.

The Island of Gorée

In this collection, I share acquired insights from people and incidents that contributed to my growing respect for these values and the wisdom of this millennial culture. These stories and memoirs somehow encapsulate some of the values upon which this culture is constructed. They are gifts from Senegal to the world, a treasure of lessons about what is important in life for anyone interested in learning to see.

CONTENTS

1

LEARNING TO SEE

<<<<<<<<<<<<<<<<<<<<<<<<<<<<<<<<<<<<<<<<<<<<<<<<

The foreigner only sees what he knows
African Proverb

There must have been 3000 people in the little neighborhood stadium that day all of whom seemed to understand what was happening, and I had absolutely no idea what was going on. I had a fair understanding of the rules of soccer or football as the beautiful game is called here in Senegal. But this was not a question of not understanding the rules. It was half time and there was no one on the field. But everybody was sharing a good laugh and getting excited about something and I had no idea what it was.

It was a cool, sunny afternoon in Dakar in the late 1960s with a breeze bearing maritime fragrances flowing from the Atlantic into the Assane Diouf stadium. In colonial times, the stadium had been called *Stade Abattoirs* (Slaughter House stadium) and had been the launching pad for many of Senegal's great runners and jumpers. In 1963, it was renamed the Stade Assane Diouf for a Senegalese boxing star of Guinean origins. Named director of Senegal's boxing team in 1963, Diouf unfortunately died soon after in a fishing accident. Many older Senegalese still called it *"Stade Abattoirs"*

A small crowd – mostly young and not so young men - had come to watch a soccer match between the local Gorée and Jaraaf teams. I was there with my friend Alpha because Pape Seck, one of our mutual Senegalese friends, played on the Gorée defense and had invited us to come see the game. Alpha was a mixture of the major Senegalese ethnic groups - Wolof, Peulh and Mandinka, with a few Serer and Diola connections further back in his ligneage - a Senegalese mosaic. He was considerably older than Pape Seck or myself but in a society where age determines status, he somehow related to younger people as equals. We, nevertheless, did observe a certain respect for his age in our interactions.

Alpha exuded faith and confidence just as his spotless white robes gave off the sweet aroma of incense. I am not sure exactly how old he was, but he had kept in shape. He had the body of a much younger man and the eyes of a visionary. He was an unending source of information about Senegal and Senegalese – one of those rare people who had been able to step out-side of his own culture and look in objectively. He was my resource person in my quest to understand this new culture, as well as a mentor and friend to me and to many others.

The first half of the match was marked with shouts of support and waves of "oohs" and "aahs" of the very excitable fans as each team almost scored but did not quite make it. My friend Pape Seck went up for a ball and clunked heads hard with another player. He was knocked out cold and car-ried off the field. All I could think of was a concussion. But by the second quarter he was back in the game showing that partic-ular resilience that characterized his life until throat cancer finally took him from us in his seventies just last year.

In Memoriam Papa Douta Seck

Otherwise, it turned out to be an uneventful half and ended in a 0 - 0 tied score to the frustration of the spectators who were hoping for something more spectacular. After the field had been completely cleared for half time, we were all mulling around or sitting in the stands quietly talking, smoking or reading newspapers. Suddenly a wave of shouting and laughing flowed over the crowd. Everyone stood and simultaneously turned pointing to the goal posts on the right. They shared high fives, slapped each other's hands and patted each other excitedly on the back and shoulders. At first, I thought the teams had come back on the field but when I looked at the goal posts where everyone was pointing, I saw nothing. The field was still empty and it was still too soon for the second half. Nothing could be seen to justify this level of excitement. Weird.

I turned to Alpha who was standing next to me, participating in the collective joy, and I said: "What the hell is going on?"

He very excitedly pointed to the goal posts like everyone else and said: "Look" as though once he called my attention to whatever it was, I would immediately understand.

I looked again at the goal posts and still saw nothing. "Don't you see them?"

By now, I was beginning to panic. "See who?"

"Not who," he said, "the two birds!"

And, yes, in fact there were two small, local red and brown sparrows called *ramatous* flying playfully in and around the goal posts. I had not even noticed them before he pointed them out.

"So what?" I said.

"Look," he said even more excitedly, "Gorée has obviously used a *gris gris* on Jaraaf and they will score in the second half just the way the birds are flying in between the goal posts! They must have a really good *marabout* for this match!"

Gorée won 2-0 and I was later to learn a lot more about the role of "*marabouts*."

I felt really stupid as I often did in those early days in Senegal. While the all pervasive influence of Islam was manifested in the prominence of mosques, the calls to prayer, the clothing people wore, I began to wonder what else of importance wasn't I seeing that was right under my nose? There was so much to learn. Alpha sort of reassured me. "A real under-standing of Senegal comes slowly in small doses and is never really com-plete for the foreigner that did not grow up here. As the African proverb says: "Foreigners have big eyes, but they only see what they know."

Walking in Dakar's Medina later that same week with Alpha, he pointed out an itinerant salesman with a little wooden and wire mesh cage packed with at least two dozen red and brown *ramatous*, the same type of

Ramatou

bird that had flown around the Jaraaf goal posts earlier in the week. As we watched, a man stopped to pur-chase one for what looked like 50 francs (10 cents).

The sales-man opened a little mesh door, reached in and took one of these tiny birds in his grip and handed it to his client. The man took the bird with two hands, whispered something and let the bird go. She flew off happily and was quickly out of sight.

The popular belief in Senegal, Alpha explained, was that this little spar-row-like bird carried your wishes to God. It was a way of asking for good fortune.

During that same week of discovery, one morning just before dawn when I had woken up early for no apparent reason, I slipped on my sneak-ers and decided to take a brisk walk around the neighborhood to get to know my surroundings and enjoy the freshness of the day. The call to prayer had just ended as the light of day was emerging, like a child timidly entering the stage for her first school play. The women of the other houses were also beginning to stir. As I walked, I noticed that my neighbor's wife, a Catholic from the south of the country called the *Casamance* was pouring cold water on the entrance stoop to her house. I greeted her without even thinking about what she was doing until I got to another house I knew. They were Moslem and Wolof from the Dakar Region. There, too, the grandmother of the family was pouring cold water on the stoop. And as I walked I noticed more and more women and young girls sleepily stepping out of their doors and pouring cold water on the front entrance to their homes before their children or grand children re-emerged to begin automatically sweeping the sidewalks or sandy roads in front of their houses with scratchy *Casamance* brooms. They spoke different languages and were obviously from different regions of the country. Since I was not used to getting up before dawn, I had never noticed this little ritual they all shared.

Later that same morning, I saw the old Peulh man setting up his little wooden table on the street in front of my door where he sold fruit - melons, bananas and oranges, candy, individual cigarettes and matches, kola nuts and enough green tea in small plastic bags for one session of *attaya*. But, early in the morning, before he started selling, he too began sprinkling water around his table from his ever-present kettle that he used for ablutions and other personal hygiene needs. I had seen that before and used to think it was meant to settle the ever-present dust around his stand. But now it took on greater significance in my eyes

I made a connection between the women in the morning and the Peulh man and figured I was on to something I did not fully understand. I began my inquiries that same afternoon with Maimouna, the young Senegalese woman who worked at my house.

"Do you pour water on the front door step of your house every morning at dawn?"

Peulh fruit seller

"Uh huh, everybody does" she responded, a little surprised by the question.

"Why do you do it?"

"It's our *aada* (tradition handed down from the ancestors)."

"But what do the older people say about it?"

"That it is a good thing to do. The cool water means your day will be cool, without problems. It protects the family and the household from *saytaane*."

"And what are *saytaane*?"

"You don't know *saytaane*?" she exclaimed incredulously. "Evil spirits that are always around us to do harm. The night belongs to them and they need to be washed away from the entrance to the home in the morning as the sun comes up."

"What kinds of harm?"

"All kinds! They cause accidents and illness and arguments for no good reason between close friends and between husbands and wives. May God protect us from them."

There was real fear in her voice.

A couple of weeks later my information was confirmed when I heard a woman commenting on a rather violent argument between a man and his wife that had spilled over into the street.

"What a shame" the woman said as she tried to calm them down.

"*Saytaane* has come between you!"

It seemed like a good pretext to eliminate the blame of either party and facilitate eventual reconciliation. It was an early version of Geraldine's phrase to avoid responsibility in Flip Wilson's TV show in the 70's: "The Devil made me do it."

Then I began to notice what was seemingly another unrelated phenomenon that I did not immediately understand. Lots of kids regularly played soccer in the big, sandy island between the double roads in front of my house that separated the neighborhood of Sicap Baobab from Sicap Amitié and Sicap Karack. Every day at one and then again at sundown their yelling would stop and an eerie silence would descend on the neighborhood, the kind that attracts your attention like a loud noise. I did not think much about it until I saw a couple of mothers angrily calling their young children to get into the house around one o'clock one day. "Late for lunch," I thought at the time.

Much later Alpha explained to me that the cracks in time at noon between morning and afternoon and at sunset, between day and night belong to the spirits and that it is important for everyone, but particularly for vulnerable people like young children and pregnant women to get out from under the trees and off the streets at that time. I am not talking about some little traditional village in the bush. I am talking about the residential areas of Senegal's cosmopolitan capital Dakar with a couple of million inhabitants!

I had seen from the beginning that Senegalese wore all sorts of amulets, many in the form of small, square leather pouches wrapped around their arms, necks, legs, waists or torsos on leather strings or attached to corn-rows in their hair with safety pins.

There were even special beads around the necks of very young children and silver bracelets with protective powers, all referred to as *gris-gris*. I learned more and more about the different types, shapes and materials of gris-gris and the different purposes they served, and about people consulting various *marabouts* or holy men quite frequently to resolve all sorts of problems they encountered.

Alpha explained that *gris-gris* contain papers with verses from the Koran, magical numbers, or mystical designs drawn by the *marabout*. "He will tell you what animal skin the *gris-gris* needs to be sewn into. While cow and goat leather are the most common, it is not uncommon to be told that you need hyena, iguana, snake, ostrich or even lion leather for specific *gris-gris* to function properly." I wondered how the hell someone in Dakar is supposed to find hyena or lion skin, until the day that Alpha took me to my first market specializing in mystical supplies and traditional pharmacopeia. I had walked by it many times without ever understanding its purpose or significance.

Gris Gris Market

These markets are spread out on animal skins or cloths on the ground along the walls of Iba Mar Diop stadium or on rickety tables in the corner or rear of major markets. Wizened old sellers sit along the wall in separate sections or stalls, protecting themselves from the sun with makeshift awnings or umbrellas. Each seller specializes in medicines for curing certain illnesses, or resolving certain problems: protection against evil spells, impotence, sexually transmitted infections, hemorrhoids, family planning, success on exams or in work, love potions and jealousy remedies, skin diseases and mental illness... And you could spend days, no years, learning about what each object is for: monkey skulls, snake grease, lizard skins, or dried monkey hands, animal bones or hair, horns from various animals, different kinds of wood in different shapes, leaves and roots, beads and multi-colored strings... I regretted not having pursued my initial ambitions to become an anthropologist when I entered college. Alpha bought a couple of objects from the sellers but did not explain to me what they were for. I thought the *gris-gris* were cool and even had a simple square leather *gri-gris* made and started wearing it around my neck to the amusement of Senegalese friends and acquaintances.

While most people wear their gris-gris discreetly, it is in Dakar's wrestling arenas that they are most evident. The much-loved wrestling match is nine-tenths mystical preparation and one-tenth wrestling. Strapped to the torsos, arms and legs of these massive opponents are the talismans created by their *marabouts* to provide magical protection. For centuries, West Africans have believed that these *gris-gris* will protect them from the spells of their enemies, and imbue them with magical strength and power. These mastodons go through all sorts of spiritual cleansing, drenched with milk or holy water, and carrying out various rituals prescribed for them to ensure their victory.

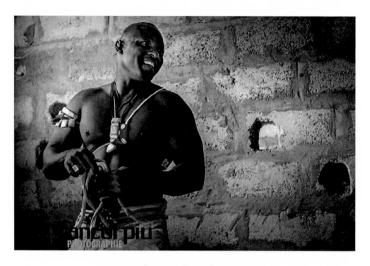

Senegalese Wrestler with Gris Gris

As I became more and more interested in this endless world of talismans and amulets, Alpha opened up and we talked more frequently about the different types of charms and how they were used to help prevent injury and death or provide cures for illness. Alpha told me about his Mandinka *marabout* uncle in Marsassoum who frequently used the written charm, encased in leather, with directions for placement on the body or medicinal instructions written in Arabic. Senegalese in general believe these gris-gris to be dangerous if worn by an enemy. A warrior in battle might wear an anti-charm to defend against them. His Mandinka uncle also used water in his protective rituals. He wrote words in Arabic on a board or paper, and the ink was then washed from it, and either drunk or washed over the body of the client. Alpha explained that you might also see someone wearing a simple string that has been blessed by the *marabout* and tied to the person, or perhaps to an animal or tree depending on the intended use. "A personal blessing by the *marabout*," he concluded, "can transform any object into medicine."

In our conversations, Alpha often mused about death in Senegal. "Death is no stranger to us. It is an ever-present reality. If it isn't a new born infant 'returning' to where he came from or a young child dying of malaria, it is a woman expiring in childbirth, several passengers killed in a horrendous *car rapide* highway accident, an old aunt suffering from diabetes whose leg was recently amputated or a patriarch whose time has come to join his ancestors." It was as though he was listing the litany of all the people he knew who had died recently.

"You once told me that in your country, if you don't live in a dangerous ghetto, you only see death once in a long while, and only after everything modern science can muster has been tried. You said that many people seem to go through life thinking that they will never die."

But in Senegal death is always very close. Many people you know well here will die or have a death in their family during your stay. Some still die of ailments long eradicated or easily treated in the West. Here death never goes away. If you don't hear about it by word of mouth, on the radio or in the newspaper, you go down a familiar street and see a large gathering of men in damask *khaftans* and women, their heads covered with large white, diaphanous scarves from Mecca, usually seated separately from the men on rented plastic chairs under a tent, silently gathering to present condolences and pay homage to a friend or relative. And you know that death has visited that home."

It seemed to me that despite or perhaps because of the frequency of visits by death, the Senegalese had developed an extraordinary empathy and capacity to cope.

To manage death and help people to cope, Senegalese culture, like other cultures, structures the mourning process. When Alpha's father died, he explained that after the burial, which for the Moslems occurs, if possible, within 24 hours of death, there were ceremonies and prayers on the third day, the eighth day and the fortieth day which correspond to the itinerary of the body and soul as they move through the stages of putrefaction and returning to their maker. Old men from the mosque are called in to read all the verses of the Coran (*wacc kamil*), following which porridge with sweet yoghurt (*laax*) and little biscuits or hard candies are distributed to all who attended. Alpha's mother, like all Moslem widows, was expected not to leave the house and to remain in mourning for four months and ten days after the death of her husband. During this period of mourning Alpha and the family took care of her needs. But after this period, she was expected to end her mourning.

Alpha explained that on the Christian side of his family they were more flexible in terms of the time between death and burial. Since his brother had married a Catholic woman, Alpha was well placed to compare Moslem and Christian customs. Catholic widows, for example, wear black for a year and do not go out after sunset. Burials are often delayed for days and sometimes weeks and bodies conserved to allow time for relatives and friends living far away to gather for the event.

If we are to believe Jeremy Rifkin, the American economic and social theorist and writer, empathy is "grounded in the acknowledgement of death and the celebration of life" and is based on our "frailties" and "imperfections."[1] Extended family and community support for the bereaved help them to cope with death. Managing an NGO later in my stay in Senegal, I learned that people here frequently take time off from work to attend funerals and burials. When a colleague loses a relative, the entire staff will form a delegation to present condolences, a practice that paralyzes operations for at least half a day. When I commented on how frustrating it was to try to run an organization when people kept taking time off for funerals, Alpha explained that most Senegalese feel a strong obligation to be present at the burial of people they have known well, or even those they have shared a neighborhood with or are somehow connected to through the intricate lacework of relationships that binds this society so tightly together. I began to see how comforting it must be to have all your colleagues come to your home in a group to share in your grief and to show your other relatives how much consideration they have for you and for the defunct..

When Moslems and some Christians present their condolences, they use an interesting Wolof phrase - "*sigindigali*" - which signifies "Remember,

---

[1] "The Empathic Civilization: The Race to Global Consciousness in a World in Crisis

you are not alone." When it is broken down it translates roughly as "Look up to see those ties that bind all of us together."

The highly organized process of presenting condolences at Catholic funerals is particularly impressive. After the burial, mourners from the tight knit Catholic community line up literally around the block and teams of designated young people manage the movement of the impressive crowds that keep coming all day long. At these moments, the solidarity of Senegal's Catholic minority is palpable.

Finally, while many attribute death and illness to some form of spiritual foul play, accepting death is intimately connected to one's faith in God. Death is seen as the person's destiny as decided by God. They often repeat the phrase *"Dogal u yallah le"* - it is the decision of God. And to encourage the grieving mourner: *"Xanaa gumulo yallah?"* "Don't you believe in God?" Your ability to cope with death is directly equated with the strength of your faith in God.

But that is not the whole story. Coexisting alongside Christian and Moslem beliefs about death is that invisible parallel universe, the world of the spirits that is as real for most Senegalese as the world Westerners see. It is a world not frequently spoken of, especially with foreigners. But when you have been here for a while, you begin to see glimpses of it all around you: the water on the doorsteps at dawn, the birds in the goal posts during half time, the children disappearing at one in the afternoon, the frequent visits to the healers and the ever-present amulets that all come together in an intricate, internally logical system.

The Senegalese perceive much danger in the world around them associated with different kinds of spirits that shadow every person and every object. Such a constant and dire threat means the *marabout* and the protection he offers, especially through amulets, is quite a serious and vital part of life. These *marabouts* range in skills from charlatans to koranic scholars and expert traditional herbalists who almost always include a spiritual dimension and some form of prayer or incantation to their healing.

Alpha introduced me to an impressive, young Western-trained Senegalese doctor. In the course of conversation about illness and traditional healing, he explained that it was estimated that over 80% of Senegalese consulted traditional healers instead of or in addition to Western medical practitioners. The doctor himself believed that certain ailments were best treated by African medicine.

Illnesses here are like familiar old enemies or unwanted relatives who come to visit. But the manifestations of these various diseases are often attributed to spirit causes rather than to germs or microbes, or physiological events such as strokes. Bell's palsy, a form of facial paralysis, for example, is attributed to having been slapped by a *djinn*. Many illnesses are attributed to spells cast by others or to imbalances caused by neglecting sacrifices to ancestors or to spirit doubles called *rabb*. Others spoke to me of evil, cannibalistic people/spirits or witches called *demm* who can eat your soul from within. Every now and then an article still appears in the newspapers about someone accused of being a *demm*, reminiscent of the witch trials of Salem.

"What do you mean when you say they are cannibals and they can eat your soul from within? I asked Alpha who was well versed in these matters.

"Have you ever bought a bunch of unshelled peanuts," he answered, "and you break open a perfectly intact shell only to find that the peanuts inside have turned to dust?"

Here as the Senegalese author Birago Diop wrote "*les morts ne sont pas morts.*" The dead are not dead. Ancestral spirits and those of the recently deceased as well are all around us and need to be placated for they intervene in the lives of the living. I only began to understand how deeply engrained all these beliefs were when I attended the viewing of the body of the daughter of a friend. I can still hear her chilling laments.

She was called Maam Helene – "grandmother Helen". She was a métisse — half French, half Diola — from the southern region of the country, the only *métisse* in a large Senegalese family that spanned regions and ethnic groups and included both Catholics and Moslems. By the time I got to know her she was already getting on in years. She always wore a head scarf as most older, married Moslem women do, and never showed her hair publicly like some other Christian women.

She was light-skinned, petite, soft spoken and polite, but had raised her kids with an iron hand. She had married a prominent Moslem doctor and had a large family with four sons and one precious daughter. Her house was filled with lace doilies and little ceramic curios and vases sort of like my grandmother's old house in Borough Park in Brooklyn many years before. A prominent picture of Jesus with his bleeding heart hung over the family dining table where all meals were served European style rather than around a common bowl as was the custom in many Senegalese homes. The children and grandchildren had been raised as Catholics. They made the sign of the cross before they ate.

Her sons were all married and the house was always filled with grandchildren playing. Her only daughter had married well and like her mother had had five kids with her Moslem husband. They were all particularly beautiful, as was their mother. But she was still young and both she and her husband felt that though they had been blessed, they did not want to have any more children. Despite her Catholic religion, they explored different contraceptive options. It was then that they learned of a recently developed procedure that was becoming very popular in the West called tubal ligation. It was an irreversible method unlike many of the others they had examined, ideal for the modern couple who were finished with child bearing. It was said to be safe, relatively simple to perform and 100% sure. Once the procedure was completed, you did not have to worry about condoms, IUDs or hormonal injections

They decided to have the procedure done in a local, private clinic belonging to a close doctor friend who had recently been to a training program in France to learn how to perform the procedure. It was one of the few clinics in Dakar to offer the service. They did not talk about it to anyone beyond the immediate family. There was clearly an element of shame in refusing God's gift of fertility.

Maam Helene's daughter left the house for the clinic telling her kids she would be home the next day. She was relaxed during pre-op preparation and probably thought about the many things they would be able to do once the procedure was completed. But due to an error in the anesthetic, Maam Helene's beautiful daughter died before the procedure had even begun, leaving five young children to be cared for by their father and her extended family who would surround them with love and attention to compensate as much as possible for their unspeakable loss.

However familiar people here are with death, and however well they cope, certain unexpected deaths are like hands suddenly tightening around the collective throat of the community, choking out its life and dreams, creating the panic of being unable to breathe, and reminding everyone that death is, in fact, inevitable and very near. These deaths really shock and mark Senegal's otherwise stoic, tight knit community: the horrible drowning of hundreds of passengers in the sinking of the Diola ferry between *Casamance* and Dakar in September 2002, the death of a popular, young father in a residential area when his vespa was side swiped by a bus, and the death of Maam Helene's beautiful, young, well-known daughter who had not even been sick, and was the living example of a fertile, life rich with unlimited possibilities for the future.

It was at the viewing of her body for close friends and family in the morgue at Le Dantec hospital that it all came together and I began to see. As expected, many people came and entered the morgue with trepidation to view the carefully prepared body when an attendant opened the heavy, squeaky iron door that dated certainly from colonial times. They sobbed and cried openly and invoked God's will. They comforted each other with hugs and encouraging words - a community united in stupefaction and deep grief. Some, clearly shaken, stepped outside to get some air or smoke a cigarette. Others sat on benches with their heads in their hands or leaning on the shoulder of a loved one.

Then, suddenly, a silence descended on those gathered when Maam Helene arrived, supported by two other older women, one on each arm. They had all known pain. It was engraved on their faces. Everyone knew Maam Helene's boundless love for her daughter that she had pampered and educated as she herself had been groomed. They all knew this was a major catastrophe. Everyone dreaded the moment when she would see her dead daughter for the first time.

She moved slowly, almost shuffling towards the body, already drained of strength by her grief and anger. When they brought her to view the body, this half white, half African, good Catholic woman did not sniffle into a handkerchief or delicately muffle her grief. She screamed the lament that welled up from somewhere deep inside her, and made me see: "They ate my child!" "They ate my child!"

2

BAL DE FIN D'ANNÉE (END-OF-YEAR DANCE)

◇◇

I f you are lucky and make it to retirement, you may well find yourself with the chance to remember and reflect on events and situations that you may not have fully understood at the time. Sometimes it is not until we look back that we begin to understand. We certainly have no idea what impact we will have on other people's lives.

Talk about "bright eyed and bushy tailed": As a Peace Corps English teacher arriving in exotic Senegal in 1965 just before the beginning of the school year, I was scheduled to teach in a Dakar *lycée* or high school, the Lycée Blaise Diagne. After a couple of years of French at Columbia and then two intensive French programs

Arriving in Senegal via Pan Am – September 1, 1965

organized by Peace Corps, my French was pretty good, relatively fluent and grammatically correct. But my mastery of the language was not as deep and rich as many of my classmates who had lived in France or another French-speaking environment. I often found myself lacking in daily vocabulary. Not having lived in French speaking Africa, I also needed to learn not only the many idiomatic expressions appropriate to West Africa but also a lot of the non-verbal gestures and sounds people in this region commonly use. I also had to learn more about the cultural underpinnings of language use and social interaction.

So looking back at how unqualified I was, it was a little surprising that when Peace Corps received an urgent request from Senegal's spanking new and prestigious Ecole Normale Supérieure built with help from UNESCO and UNDP to improve teacher training and gradually replace expatriate teachers with trained Senegalese, the Peace Corps Director asked me if

My first view of the spanking new Ecole Normale Supérieure 1965

I would be willing to teach in the Teacher's College. A key Belgian technical assistant had fallen ill just before the beginning of the school year, and the Ministry of Education was scrambling to find a qualified replacement – or even a partially qualified replacement – to fill this key position for the training of Senegalese English teachers.

While I was among the most fluent French speakers in my group and had already begun learning Wolof, one of the major national languages, I did not feel qualified and was too young and inexperienced to question the moral and ethical implications of providing only partially qualified technical assistants. Were we really better than nothing?

I was encouraged to take on the challenge convinced by arguments that my fluency in English and the language teaching techniques I had acquired during Peace Corps training would make up for any lack of experience. So I found myself assigned to the ENS with First and Second Year English teacher candidates as well as a light schedule in the high school level practice school incorporated into the teacher's college.

In May 1961, soon after many African countries achieved independence, a meeting was held in Addis Abeba under the shared auspices of UNESCO and the Economic Commission for Africa (UNDP), the first meeting of African States on the development of Education in Africa. The work of this meeting later proved to be of great importance for the development of education, social progress and the validation and application of the cultural richness of Africa to the challenge of economic and social development.

One of the results envisaged by the conference was that the Special UN Fund (UNDP) working through UNESCO, would come to the aid of African countries that wished to create national institutes for the training of secondary school teachers. The assistance of the Special Fund over a period of 6 to 8 years would mainly take the form of assistance by foreign professors or "experts", didactic equipment (language labs and libraries) and study scholarships for national professors who would gradually replace foreign experts. For their part, governments would have to provide a working budget, ensure necessary construction and name national candidates who, after additional training financed by scholarships from the special fund, (UNDP), would return to the establishment to ensure replacement of the experts in the teaching chairs in their specialties.

From 1961, 20 national teacher training schools were created each with its own characteristics taking into account the realities, needs, resources and objectives of the country but unified beyond the diversity of national condition, languages and structures with a shared vocation and spirit. In 1962 The Advanced Pedagogic center of Dakar was created and renamed the Ecole Normale Supérieure of Dakar in 1964 – that benefitted from international assistance for the following seven years.

The Director and teaching staff of the ENS and the practice school were mostly European technical assistants: French, Swiss and Belgians. While they were cordial, I now understand that they viewed my as a young, unqualified interloper who had not earned his stripes. Except for Prof. Sequaris, an older, heavy-set avuncular teacher of psycho-pedagogy who immediately understood my predicament, took a liking to me and sort of took me under his wing. He invited me to his home every couple of weeks where his wife cooked delicious, copious meals with lots of butter and eggs

Gary Engelberg circa 1965

and potatoes. She reminded me of my grandmother. Their love and support certainly helped me get through that challenging first year. I made up for my lack of experience in teaching with enthusiasm and creativity.

On my first day I discovered that my first and second year English teacher students were about my age. A couple were a bit older, were married and had children. I had the advantage of being an unusual entity, a nice looking young, white American, fluent in English who spoke a little Wolof, full of enthusiasm and a sense of mission. This did not fully make up for my inexperience, and I still cringe when I think of my awkwardness and numerous faux pas during my first months. But I genuinely liked my teacher trainee students and my sense was that they forgave my ineptitude and enjoyed my unique, less formal approach to teaching as well. Our classes were fun and filled with passionate debates in English, laughter and healthy humor.

At the time I did not think about how important these young English teacher candidates would become, many of them going to the top of the education hierarchy of the country and others going beyond education to excel in other national fields and international organizations thanks, in part, to their mastery of English. Many of them became life long friends. Let me tell you about a few of them.

Teaching at the Ecole Normale Supérieure

It was 1965 and the Vietnamese war was heating up. To avoid the draft, many of us opposed to the war sought medical exemptions, fled to Canada or became involved in alternative service. Although Peace Corps was no guarantee that we would not be drafted. I guess I was lucky. On my fist day of class, I found myself in front of a small class of five men and two women. One of the students was J.S., a lovely, gentle, soft spoken Vietnamese woman from Hanoi. I later learned that because of Senegal's role in the French empire many Senegalese soldiers had fought at Dien Bien Phu in Vietnam and, if they survived, had returned home with Vietnamese wives. In fact, there was an entire community of Senegalo-Vietnamese families and their offspring in Dakar. J.S had come to Senegal with her Senegalese husband, Colonel S. and had founded a family. She had returned to school to get a degree so that she could return to teaching now that her children were growing.

So there I was leading an ice-breaking exercise on "getting to know you", a young anti-war American faced perhaps for the first time in my life, with a real live North Vietnamese person who had undoubtedly been affected by the terrible Vietnamese war. After she finished her presentation, I could not go on without saying to her how sorry I was about the policy of my country towards her country. She began to cry and I felt like crawling under a desk as a couple of the Senegalese students glared at me and one even said " You see?" as though I was responsible for the war.

The moment passed and I pushed on with the class, but it took me a while to feel comfortable again. Ironically, J.S. and I became good friends over the years and even got to talk about our first exchange. She claimed that she had had a baby not long before the beginning of school, was very nervous about the class and had left Vietnam many years ago. She attributed her tears to her state of mind rather than to grieving about the war. Over the years, I got to know her husband and her lovely children, who in turn became life long friends. Her husband turned out to be the uncle a man who was to become one of best friends. It never ceases to surprise me, how tightly Senegalese society is woven together, how everyone is related and how even foreigners can be integrated into the social fabric as full members. Sadly, years after our meeting at their first English class at the ENS, J.S. tragically died in childbirth. She left a gaping hole in her community of family and friends and her death was one of the most deeply felt losses I experienced in Senegal.

The other woman in the class was the most beautiful, charming M.F. She was of mixed Senegalese and Moroccan origins and was light-skinned with long straight hair. She was present for the first few days of classes always wearing elegant, flowing Senegalese boubous rather than Western dress. Her participation in class was always smart, provocative and filled with humor. She disappeared from class one day early on in the term and did not reappear until several months later to present us with her beautiful new son and rejoin the class. I had not even noticed that she was pregnant.

M.F. went on to work for UNESCO and became the UNESCO Country Representative to both Jordan and then Canada.

A. N. was a slim, young, handsome, light-skinned Peulh from Velingara in the south of the country. He was the one who got on my case when J.S. had cried. But we, too, eventually became friends. He was always the firebrand of the class. He married and had a child with J.G., a Peace Corps Volunteer and eventually moved to Washington and worked for the IMF. A.N.'s life was saved, as I understand it, when a routine medical exam related to getting a visa to travel between the US and Canada, revealed a hole in his heart. He was operated on in the US and went on to live a healthy life. If he had been in Senegal, the anomaly might not have been identified, and he probably would have died young, suddenly, and people would have thought that someone had cast a spell on him. I learned that he and his wife had later divorced and that he had left the IMF. Unfortunately, we have lost touch and sadly, I do not know what became of him.

Small of stature, athletic, with huge, sad eyes, N.N. was loved by all. He had a magnetic personality – what the Senegalese call *"bayré"* - a great sense of humor and a quick smile. He turned out to be great friend. I was by his side when he buried a young woman who had died in childbirth with his illegitimate child, a shock that he never recovered from. I recommended him to go to Peace Corps training in the US as a language instructor to work with PC volunteers in the summer. He was chosen and brought to the US to teach for Peace Corps. He was a brilliant teacher. Unfortunately, he did not come back for many years.

I got lots of criticism from colleagues. They saw N.N. as a ten-year investment in the Senegalese school system by contractual arrangement and felt that I had deprived Senegal of a valuable resource. He had two successive marriages to two African American women and had a beautiful daughter. Unfortunately, he went on to have a psychotic break and heard voices in his head controlling him. He was afraid to look people in the eye for fear that these beings in his head would transfer to his friends though eye contact and they too would suffer from what he was suffering from. He finally committed suicide in the US probably because he could no longer stand the pain; another loss that sent shock waves through the community.

Since Senegal was only a few years after independence and still training and recruiting people to run the new country, the trained teachers coming out of the ENS were to go on to become leaders of the new Senegal. A student teacher in my second year class, Mamadou Kandji, went on to become head of the British Council in Dakar and chairman of the University of Dakar English Department.

Another student in the Department of History and Geography was named Iba Der Thiam. He was a vociferous, left leaning union leader and went on to become a well-known writer, historian, and politician. He was imprisoned under President Léopold Sédar Senghor for

Iba Der Thiam

attempting to organize the country's intellectuals. Under President Abdou Diouf, he served in the government as Minister of National Education from 1983 to 1988; later, he was First Vice-President of the National Assembly of Senegal from 2001 to 2012. He has had a rich and varied career in politics, created a national political party, was candidate for President of Senegal and is currently a Deputy in Senegal's National Assembly.

But in addition to the students, I found myself in the company of a man who, without my knowing it, was to become one of Senegal's senior moral leaders and a Director General of UNESCO at the center of the debate on the New World Information and Communication Order and the battle between UNESCO and the USA.

Amadou Mahtar M'Bow is a Senegalese educator born in Dakar in 1921. He served in France and North Africa during World War II after volunteering for the French army. After the end of the war he studied geography at the Sorbonne University in Paris. M'bow began working for UNESCO in 1953 and came to the ENS in the 60's to head the Department of History and Geography. His lovely wife, Raymonde, was head of the ENS Documentation Center and his son, Fara, was my student in the practice school.

He was one of the few faculty at the ENS who was welcoming and supportive to this awkward but well-meaning young American Peace Corps teacher. We would speak occasionally, he would ask me how I was doing, but we never became very close. Nevertheless, I had great respect and affection for him. I wish now that I had spent more time with him. He left the ENS in 1966 to become Senegal's Minister of Education until 1968. The students and faculty of the ENS were particularly proud that the minister had come from their ranks and saw him as "their Minister."

He went on to become Senegal's Minister of Youth and Culture from 1968 to 1970 and Deputy to Senegal's Assembly. By 1980 he had become the first Black African General Director of UNESCO, a post that he occupied until 1987. Under his direction, the Sean MacBride report, *Many Voices, One World* presented recommendations for establishing a new more equitable world order of information and communication.

Amadou Mahtar Mbow

During this difficult Cold War period, as Secretary General of UNESCO, Mbow fought to maintain the cohesion of his Member States around the ideals of the organization favoring open debate, consultation and decision making based on consensus. He worked tirelessly to open the organization to the realities of the world, ensure mutual comprehension among people through shared understanding of each other's cultures, progress and renovation in the field of education, development of knowledge and international cooperation in technical, social and human sciences, communication and information. He tried to ensure the respect for human rights in the fields within the UNESCO mandate in collaboration with the member States and intellectuals from different regions of the world. Under Mbow, Third World participation in the organization increased markedly.

In 1984, the Government of the United States announced its intention to withdraw from UNESCO, and withdraw its support from the organization. They felt Mbow had turned UNESCO into a vehicle of anti-American propaganda. He finally withdrew from UNESCO in 1987 as a condition for the return of the US to the organization.

Towards the end of my first year at the ENS in May 1966, I received an invitation to a *"Bal de Fin d'Année"* - an end of year dance organized by the students. They invited and requested the support of all faculty members. I loved my students, loved Senegalese music and loved to dance, and was proud to have mastered Afro-Cuban dancing to an extent, though less so Senegalese dancing. I invited Linda, an attractive Peace Corps Volunteer who shared my taste for dancing, and we appeared neatly dressed in our best threads at the ENS restaurant where the dance was being held.

The Senegalese women were all very elegant with intricate braids or wigs, heavily made up and dressed to the nines with long, often sparkly gowns. Linda was simpler with a clear, healthy complexion without makeup, dirty blond hair pulled back in a simple pony tail and wearing a simple, knee length cotton party dress that showcased her small breasts, slim, athletic figure and long, shapely legs.

Instead of the usual restaurant configuration of furniture, all the tables and chairs in the large rectangular room that housed the school's refectory had been placed up against three sides of the room with places for seating and serving the evening's snacks and soft drinks with all chairs facing the center. The room seemed enormous with a big open space in the middle for dancing. Lots of little kids stood outside the louvre windows peering in to watch the festivities. On the far side of the room a three level wooden platform had been built to house the live band that was already providing entertainment in the form of lively French, Afro-Cuban and Senegalese rhythms. The sounds of "El Manisero" pulsed through the room.

We entered and were greeted warmly by a student hostess who placed us at the head table where all the teachers were sitting. The tables were covered with little plates of snacks and bottles of soft drinks and cups. We were a bit early and took the time to greet people and appreciate the lively music, as faculty and students trickled in and seated themselves around the room. Time is very elastic in Senegal and nothing ever starts on time.

We made small, polite talk with the faculty members in our immediate vicinity, talked quietly between us remarking on the great music and how beautifully the Senegalese women were dressed, and gradually fell into silence, staring at the empty dance floor.

After a while we began to get restless and did not understand why people were not dancing. "Maybe they're shy" said my partner. So we waited some more, tapping our feet waiting for things to get started. "Do you think if we get up to dance the other's will follow and we can get this thing off the ground?" We waited a bit longer, and finally decided to dance. I leaned over to the middle aged, French expert, Mme. Braunn (pronounced "Brown"), sitting to my left, dressed in French elegance, her expensive perfume wafting around her, and said "We're going to dance." "Très bien" she responded with a smile and a nod.

So I rose with my partner and we moved onto the dance floor hoping that others would follow. Nobody moved. So we began to execute our best steps to show our hosts how well we had done in learning how to dance in Senegal. Who says white people don't have rhythm?

I can't tell you how long our dance lasted but it felt like an eternity as we kept waiting for others to join us. The band increased the speed of the music and ended their song with a great drum solo. We stopped, applauded the band, nodded to each other, smiled and moved back to our seats content and a bit out of breath. There was scattered applause in the room. Not very enthusiastic. Mme. Braunn smiled and nodded as we took our places.

The band continued playing and still, nobody moved. About fifteen minutes later there was some commotion at the front door and Amadou Mahtar Mbow, who had recently been named Minister of Education and his wife Raymonde, entered the room. They shook hands with those in their immediate vicinity, smiled and waved and greeted everyone and were seated at a special table in the front of the room. They received a warm ovation, were served something to drink and then rose to officially open the *"bal de fin d'année"* with a dance.

3

MATY'S NEW FRIEND

◇◇

I n 1974, I watched an unlikely friendship blossom between two women from very different cultures.

Carole (with an e) Berlinski had demystified just about everything. She was a 45-year old psychologist from D.C. whose clients were mostly gay men. She had been raped as a young woman, married, and divorced and had been through a series of unsatisfying relationships leading to her current restlessness. She was still active and attractive and felt a need to discover new places and try new and different relationships. She needed to step out of the monotony and loneliness of her life.

Despite all she had been through, she was surprisingly joyful and personable. With her warm smile and ready laugh, she adapted well to new situations and new people and easily established superficial but mutually satisfying friendships. She was the kind of person you would meet at a cocktail party over a gin and tonic and might remember but never see again.

Like lots of us she was searching for the meaning of things: life, relationships, God and death. She dabbled in meditation, Eastern religions, rediscovered her Jewish heritage and not finding the answers she was looking for, gradually gave up the active search. But the question marks remained somewhere inside her mind, body, soul or spirit – wherever it is that we store our unresolved issues.

When she received an invitation from an old, gay friend to visit him in Africa, in the former French colony of Senegal where he was working in AIDS prevention and reproductive health, she did not hesitate. She had the means and was mistress of her time. She rescheduled all her appointments. How many times would she be lucky enough to have a good friend to host her in such an exotic place? Passport, shots, ticket and she found herself waking up just as the RK50 Air Afrique flight touched down in Dakar at 5:35 in the morning, Dakar time.

It was still the cool season in Dakar in early May but the humidity and the new aromas hit her immediately as she descended the steps to the tarmac into a rickety French-made bus that carried her and the other passengers to the terminal. They were a mixture of tired but chatty American tourists in shorts and sneakers, a few marginal men and women with strange haircuts and unusual clothing, a number of tall, elegant Senegalese men, and many colorful Senegalese women with lots of bags. And of course the four or five beautiful children with huge dark eyes and bright, smiles itching to run and restrained by their mothers.

Because two other flights had landed at the same time, the small airport was packed with impatient in-coming passengers from different countries. The noise level in the terminal building was high, the sounds of different languages confusing, the lines interminable and the police and customs agents overwhelmed. But she had learned in life that with patience you can get through anything, no matter how unpleasant. And soon she found herself at the beginning of her adventure in a charming new city glimmering under the rising African sun.

In a little two-room house in a suburb of Dakar called SICAP Liberté 4, Maty Sow was up for the morning prayer. As she did every day, she remembered sadly when she would pray standing behind her husband Tapha and how he used to go back to bed after prayers while she continued to organize the house. And this day was no different. She poured cold water on her doorstep and woke her daughters, but not her son, in the other room that served as bedroom and living room. She did not have to give them instructions. They sleepily picked up their brooms and automatically began sweeping the courtyard raising clouds of dust. The traditional Casamance brooms produced a rhythmic scratch as her daughter Peinda progressed across their little concrete yard in the back and Awa swept up the dead leaves and powdered milk wrappers on the sandy road right in front of their house.

The two girls created a rhythmic Senegalese stereo repeated simultaneously in houses around the neighborhood. The morning symphony was punctuated by roosters crowing, little children crying and the fronds of the palms rattling like rain in the gentle morning wind that carried the smell of the ocean.

Maty and Tapha had been desperately poor. They had somehow managed to live on Tapha's meagre civil servant's salary and anything Maty could manage to generate using her ease of communication and her vast network of family, friends and acquaintances. Each day was a struggle. But she was happy - a happiness she had earned by thwarting tradition. She had married Tapha, the younger, shy but handsome bachelor she loved after leaving her wealthy husband of 18 years. Scandal! Friends told her she was crazy to sacrifice the security that so many women sought. There had been rumors of infidelity but she always denied that anything had happened between her and Tapha before she left her husband. She now lived the silent rejection of her new husband's family on a daily basis. Nobody liked the slightly older divorcee and nobody in the family would help her. But coming out of a violent and unhappy first marriage, she felt like she had landed in paradise.

Her first husband had been a relatively rich businessman who gave her everything but love. His sporadic violence and serial infidelity became part of her reality. When she finally left him, she was not used to the poverty she found with her new husband, Tapha. She found herself doing the tasks that were done by her maids in her previous marriage. But she never complained. She was clever and found ways of making ends meet. And Tapha was gentle and loved her. And when she was able to bear three more children for her Tapha - a boy and two girls – despite being late in life for childbearing, she thanked God and gladly coped with the economic pressures the children brought. She was a devoted, understanding mother and her kids adored her. Her happiness was complete.

But that happiness ended abruptly one morning when Tapha, who had always had problems with high blood pressure, grabbed his head and collapsed in the bathroom of their home when he was preparing for morning prayer. Maty silently cradled him in her arms speaking to him quietly and praying that he would survive until the ambulance from the nearby fire department arrived to take him to the hospital. It was only then that she began to wail.

Tapha was dead on arrival due to a massive stroke and buried within 24 hours according to Moslem custom. In less than one day, after only eight years of marriage, Maty was transformed into a grieving widow with four and a half months of compulsory confinement and mourning before her, and three children to raise alone.

But Maty's life was not over. Even widowhood could not kill her vibrant spirit. She was a full breasted, broad hipped, woman with the large, high buttocks that Senegalese men loved, and she remained lithe and graceful in her movements. She had been known for her prowess as a dancer and had always been anxiously awaited by the other neighborhood women when they organized a *sabaar* and showered her with money when she danced. When she came out of mourning, though her heart was no longer in it, she danced because she needed to exploit every possibility to earn money to support her children. In happier times, she had also been a master of *tassou*, a traditional, often risqué, form of traditional poetry recited during street dances among women and accompanied by the beat of the tam tam, ending in a frenetic dance:

When you go to sleep at night,

And hear the bed next door creak,

Don't ask yourself who's making

The bed springs creak.

It's the owner of the bed

Who is making it creak.

Creak, he's thrusting his hips,

Creak he's thrusting his hips...

Her dancing skills had been honed in her childhood. As a young girl, Maty had been strikingly beautiful. Light skinned with straight, dark shiny hair thanks to her Mauritanian/Peulh heritage, she attracted attention right from the beginning. At 14, with budding breasts and a flashing smile, she had collected and saved the silver dollars thrown into the circle of the street dances by the American soldiers who occupied Dakar at the end of the war and gathered to watch the beautiful, young women do their erotic moves. A number of young women of her generation had their silver dollar collection that they kept as souvenirs of their prime. They only used them when they encountered financial difficulties in their adult lives. By the time Carole Berlinski met Maty, she had only three silver dollars left.

After an exciting week in Senegal, Carole was invited to a Senegalese lunch at the home of a friend of her host that I was lucky enough to attend. There she met Maty. Though they had very little language in common, Carole and Maty immediately recognized that they were kindred spirits. By the end of the meal eating rice with their hands around a common bowl, they found themselves relaxing on pillows on a woven mat in the back yard, drinking tea and laughing hysterically at their sign language, broken English, broken French often off-color jokes.

They did not need words to communicate. As women do, they admired each others' hair, clothes and jewelry and particularly their earrings, noting with pleasure that they also had pierced ears in common. They both enjoyed bawdy humor and began to let down their guards. Carole somehow communicated to Maty that she had gone off with a nice, young Senegalese man she met at her friend's house who unfortunately was not very satisfying sexually because he had a "needle dick" as she held up her pinky. Laughter. Maty, in return, shared with Carole that her husband had been well endowed, holding up her forearm and making a fist, and that he had been quite active in bed as she rocked her hips back and forth in the internationally understood code for sex. More laughter.

But as the afternoon went on, Maty also occasionally asked us for assistance to communicate certain more complicated vocabulary: how unhappy she had been in her first marriage, the story of the untimely death of her second husband and the emptiness she felt when she reached out to touch him in her sleep and found his side of the bed to be empty. With the help of her friends, she explained how she had treated her new husband like her child, placing cool compresses on his forehead when he had malaria, gently scratching his head as he was falling asleep and even blowing on his anus to relieve the pain of his hemorrhoids. But she could not save him from the stroke that tore him away from her. She also described being left destitute and the struggle to provide for her children that kept her going. As the conversation continued and the complicity grew between the two women, Carole popped her own psychological abscess, and revealed that she had been raped as a young woman and talked about her unhappy marriage as well. By the end of the afternoon, they were sisters.

When they parted company after the three cups of increasingly sweet and minty *attaya*, traditional Senegalese tea, that ended the leisurely lunch, they embraced warmly with more smiles and laughter and promised they would keep in touch. Maty said she would come by to see Carole again before she left - promises often made in similar situations but rarely kept.

We all helped Carole organize a trip to Senegal's *Petite Côte* tourist complex, where she had a typical tourist experience basking in the sun but not swimming in the ocean because the water was still too cold. She made several organized excursions to tourist sites, had her hair braided African style and looked a lot better than many other foreign women with African hair styles; she bought a couple of pieces of colorful Dutch Wax material and had new dresses sewn with one of the many available tailors near the hotels. She sat for hours talking to the sellers and tailors, drinking tea and eating the ever-present *gerte caff* (peanuts roasted in hot sand over coals) she was offered wherever she went. She had a one-night stand with one of the handsome, muscular, younger Senegalese men who haunt the tourist sites looking for older European or American women to take them away from Senegal. Before she returned to Dakar, she leisurely bargained for a few locally made gifts for friends in the U.S. In short, she was well received wherever she went and had a great time. She began to feel and appreciate the warmth of Senegalese *teranga* (hospitality) as well as the elasticity of Senegalese time.

On her way back to Dakar, she arranged for a half day at Senegal's Bandia animal preserve. What was a trip to Africa without a safari? She loved the colorful birds, the different species of antelope and, of course the giraffes. She was impressed by the massive rhino and disappointed with the sleepy old crocodiles around the water hole. The screeching monkeys made her day as did a surprisingly spiritual visit to a huge, hollow baobab tree where the Sereer traditionally buried their *griots* – African minstrels and oral historians attached to different families who could recite their lineage and recount the exploits of their ancestors going back to the 12th century!

Carole wondered about her own ancestors and where they might have come from originally. She remembered her great aunts and uncles who had been killed in the holocaust. They had been gassed and incinerated or thrown naked and emaciated into common graves and covered with quicklime and dirt shoveled by other prisoners and guards. Being buried in the trunk of a majestic baobab seemed a more dignified end of life, she thought.

The Baobab burial and the rapidly approaching end to this fabulous trip made her think about endings. She wondered where and how her own body would be disposed of when she died and who would come to her funeral, but she was pulled away from her dark musings by the cries of the monkeys swinging from the trees. Instead of leaving Bandia feeling invigorated by her visit to the preserve, she found herself feeling sad and lonely on the ride back, and needing to connect with someone who cared about her with whom she could unload the avalanche of thoughts and impressions that had begun flooding her mind since she arrived in Senegal.

At Carole's farewell dinner back in Dakar the day before her scheduled departure, Maty appeared as promised, to Carole's utter delight. They embraced as though they had not seen each other for years. Carole had so much to tell her and show her. Maty listened, nodded and smiled as Carole talked. They laughed together as they had on the first day they met.

As the evening progressed, their discussions turned serious as Maty sensed a deep sadness, a desperate loneliness in her American friend. She held her hand and at one point called me over to translate as she told Carole about her own life, occasionally letting a tear escape. She asked me to tell Carole about her conviction that we have to rise to the challenges that God places in our path. She wanted to be sure the Carol(e) had understood what she was saying, like a doctor verifying that her patient had understood her instructions. Coming from a woman who had survived so many challenges, this had special meaning for Carole. She knew that Maty understood her loneliness. Her mood lightened as she sat and listened to Maty until she could barely feel that sore place that she always carried within her buried under smiles and laughter.

Maty rose to leave. She declined Carole's invitation to stay for dinner saying she had to get back to the house to prepare the children for school the next day. It was clear that she did not want to be present for that painful last goodbye. As she was leaving, she offered a more relaxed, newly-tanned, newly-tressed, African clad Carole with an 'e' something folded in a little tissue paper package. Carole excitedly opened this totally unexpected gift. In the crisp sheets of white and purple tissue paper, she found a pair of sparkling filigreed silver earrings expertly crafted by a local artisan. She immediately took off the earrings she was wearing and replaced them with Maty's gift. With tears in her eyes, she hugged Maty warmly before they separated for the last time with great difficulty as though they were stuck together by chewing gum.

Having witnessed the evolution of this unlikely friendship, and knowing Maty's precarious financial situation, I wanted to see how she was doing and was curious to know how she had found the means to buy such expensive silver earrings for Carole. Weeks later, on a hot, sticky Dakar evening I visited Maty in her little three-room house. The linoleum on her cement floors was old and cracking and there were piles of termite dust at the bottom of the wooden door frames. I brought her a picture post card of D.C. with greetings from Carole that elicited a delighted reaction. In the course of conversation, I complemented her on the lovely gift she had offered Carole and diplomatically asked how she managed it. She looked at me with one of her special smiles and said she had given the jeweler her last three silver dollars to melt down and transform…

"But those silver dollars were so important to you, and you knew Carole for such a short time…" I said. She responded simply in Wolof: "Xool dey gissé" ("Hearts can see each other").

4

FADEL

◇◇◇

*Ravens are members of the crow family, easily recognized by their
massive size, their all black color, their large bill and long wings and
their diamond shaped tail when they are seen in flight...*

September 2005 - Several older men in flowing white robes waited their turn to wash their hands with water from an old kettle placed on a stone at the entrance to the cemetery. Fadel looked back on the dusty graveyard behind them where they had just buried his wife. There were several recent graves covered with sticks as was the custom among the pious *Haalpulaar or Toucouleur, Fulaanis* of northern Senegal. As he waited his turn to wash his hands, it occurred to him that the graves looked like the nests of some massive black birds of prey.

Fadel was young but he was not well. He had returned to his native *Fouta Toro,* the Region of origin of Iman El Hadj Oumar Tall, a West African political leader, Islamic scholar, and Toucouleur military commander who founded a brief empire in the 1800's encompassing much of what is now Guinea, Senegal, and Mali. Fadel had come back to care for his young, ailing wife. He had not come back in time to bury his baby daughter who had died months earlier, a daughter he had never seen alive. It was his second trip back from the Congo where he had gone six years before as a young man to make his fortune. Farming was no longer profitable in the cracked earth of their drought-ridden region. He was nineteen at the time and the stories of the lush forests and strange customs of central Africa had piqued his curiosity. Like the young Massai man in East Africa who kills his first lion, it had been time for Fadel to go off and prove that he was a man capable of supporting his family.

The mining industry of the Democratic Republic of the Congo or Zaire as it was known at the time, was rich in natural resources. It was estimated to have trillions of dollars worth of untapped deposits of raw mineral ores, including the world's largest reserves of cobalt and significant quantities of the world's diamonds, gold and copper. It attracted traders from all over Africa.

Many West Africans served as middle men between the small artisanal operators extracting diamonds and gold selling at a profit to some of the larger mining groups or to the Lebanese and Greek merchants. They invested their profits into the purchase of goods also sold at a mark up and circulated among the network of other traders from their country. A young man could make quite a bit of money in a relatively short time if he lived frugally. It was a lot more money than Fadel could have earned working in the northern regions of Senegal where unemployment was high and agriculture virtually impossible.

The first three years in Kabila's Congo had been the most difficult and, at the same time, the freest, most invigorating time Fadel had ever known. He had had to learn to fend for himself. But released from the strict social constraints of his traditional Moslem *Haalpulaar* community he had tasted another forbidden life: warm beer, throbbing music and big-breasted women with bright red lips, short skirts and rotating hips that rubbed against him as they danced. In clouds of alcohol and smoke, he became another man, living, if only temporarily, by another set of rules.

He learned to dance to the sounds of Papa Wemba and Koffi Olomide. It was like trying on a new shirt he knew he would never wear in his village, but liking the tight feel of the sheer material against his skin and the way it highlighted his slim, muscular body.

He remembered his first joyful return to his village after three years. The dust in the bumpy old Peugeot 404 taxi seemed to find every opening between the hot metal panels and the flapping canvas sidings tied down with rope through reinforced eyelets. The women in the bush taxi with him had covered their heads with their diaphanous white scarves from Mecca. He had bound his head and face in a blue turban in the style of the Maures who shared his region on the northern border of Senegal with Mauritania.

Despite the crowded taxi, the stifling heat, the uncomfortable wooden benches and the swirling dust, he could still remember how pleased he had been to return to his village with enough money and gifts to complete the formalities and consummate his marriage to Salimata. The older women accompanied his taxi when he arrived ululating and walking with him to his house waving their scarves. Salimata had been given to him as his wife a year before he left when she was only fourteen. Now she was almost eighteen. He would bring his new wife to live in his mother's compound, and she would bear his children and help his mother when he returned to the Congo to continue his trading.

Toucouleur Village

He stayed in the village for eight months, until he was sure that his wife was carrying his child. Then he made the rounds to say goodbye to each member of his extended family before he retraced the same route he had taken three years earlier. This time he was not quite so anxious to go. Salimata was beautiful and he loved the feel of her velvet skin and warm, lithe body next to his, but that was only part of what was pulling at his heart. He felt comfortable with her.

They both knew the rules, they both knew what was expected of each of them, and they both did their best to meet everyone's expectations. And as a reward, they were respected. When something was not clear, there was always an uncle or a grandmother to explain what should be done. And then there was the child to be born. His first. And he probably would not get back until the baby was two years old. Now he was going to make enough money to provide for her and the other children to come, God willing. *Nsha'allah.*

As the *taxi brousse* pulled out of the village, he thought with a twinge of shame of the outdoor *maquis* in the Congo where he would sneak away from his little *Haalpulaar* community from time to time to drink beer and spend time with Agnes.

While his relations with Salimata felt ordained and established, his liaison with the Congolese woman was forbidden fruit, exciting in its spontaneity. They constantly surprised each other with their unexpected reactions. Despite the shame he felt, despite his marriage, despite the constant reminders by relatives and friends of who he was and who he should become, part of him could not wait to see Agnes. With Agnes, there was no shame, only *joie de vivre*.

Fadel was surprised at the vacillations of his mind. How could two such different people be housed in the same body? Who was the real Fadel? The tall, reserved, proud *Haalpulaar* or the young, adventurous foreigner, hungry for new experiences?

After a long trip filled with delays, he finally arrived back in the Congo. The trip upriver from Kinshasa was uneventful and his reintegration into the little *Haalpulaar* community was filled with brotherly smiles, repeated handshakes, long discussions about their village in the Fouta, praying together, and endless cups of *attaya* (sweetened green tea with mint).

After a respectful few days of full attendance, he gradually found the time to slip away alone to the *maquis*. His Congolese friends were happy to see him and greeted him warmly, shouting, hugging, backslapping. The Zairois were so effusive. But when he asked for Agnes they became quiet, looked down at the ground and told him she was no longer there. She had been sick and had gone back to the village. No, they did not know when she would be back. The look in their eyes when they responded made him uneasy. It was as though they knew something they did not want to say. As he left the bar that night, a large black bird with a diamond-shaped tail, startled by the slamming gate, flew off screeching into the night.

About a year later, he woke up to a week of hell. He had not been feeling well for some time and had even missed going to the market on Monday. His illness felt like the onset of malaria, but never seemed to go away. On

Tuesday he learned that Agnes had died and been buried in her village. On Thursday he got a call from Senegal saying that his little eleven-month old daughter had died and that his wife, Salimata, was very ill. They urged him to come back immediately. Everyone contributed to his airfare and by Saturday he was on a plane to Senegal. He returned to his village silently grieving for Agnes, heartsick that he had never seen his daughter and deeply worried about his young wife. He cared for Salimata for over a year until she, too, died and was buried.

The men continued back to the family compound from the cemetery where Fadel's mother and other women were seated on mats, veiled and waiting in silence. Condolences were expressed, ceremonies performed, prayers said. Time passed and Fadel, always weak and tired, began nevertheless to plan his third return to the Congo. He would spend another few years there, then he would come home to resume village life. But a week before his planned departure, his uncle and his father-in-law came to announce that he would marry Daba, Salimata's younger sister. The only way to get over what had happened, they told him, was to marry again and have another child.

Fadel did as he was told, as he was expected to, as things should be. He waited several months longer than he had planned before finally leaving the village. His aging mother came out of her hut, walking with difficulty to pour water from an old kettle onto the wheels of the car that would carry him away.

Fadel left his new wife standing at the gate of their compound, pregnant, waving good-bye. This time, as the taxi left the village, the voyage that lay before him seemed impossible. He was so tired, and the trip was so long. He somehow knew he would not come back. Out of the corner of his eye, he thought he saw a large black bird perched on the straw roof of his hut.

By the time news of Fadel's death in the Congo reached the Fouta, the community had begun requiring HIV testing before proceeding with the inheritance of the wife of a deceased brother or replacement of a deceased sister in her marriage. When returning migrant workers were involved, the family insisted on an HIV test before giving the hand of their daughter in marriage. So too came the treatment to help prevent transmission of HIV from mother to child.

In Fadel's Fouta Toro, with the spread of the HIV epidemic, many communities became increasingly aware of the risk of HIV transmission. Government efforts and, more particularly, activities by dedicated community-based organizations contributed to this growing awareness. This came too late for Fadel whose death in the Congo was followed by the miscarriage of his second wife and her subsequent death.

The many clusters of tragic losses in young families such as Fadel's had reached beyond the couple into the extended family through wife inheritance and mother-to-child transmission decimating entire clans. Where information alone had failed to change practices, life experience succeeded. This very traditional community maintained its traditions, until, based on empirical knowledge, they finally understood the threats of AIDS and adapted to them.

With the help of medical authorities, they grafted modern medical tools and procedures such as condoms and HIV testing onto their traditional practices to ensure their survival as a community. Work continued on raising awareness and providing greater access to the testing, counseling, care and support services needed.

In this arid zone of high migration and proud, pious people, traditional communicators joined in the response to the epidemic. The story of a man modeled on Fadel and his family was told and retold by griots across generations as a way to convince young skeptics and prepare them for their responsibilities to the community as they followed Fadel's traces to earn enough money to pay the bride price for their lovely, new wives — this in the hope that they would do as they were told, as they were expected to do, as things should be…

5

RETURN OF THE MIGRANT

◇◇

*Thousands of Africans have attempted to migrate to Europe in order
to find work and provide for their families...*

I n the seven years since Lamine had left Senegal, both his mother and his
older brother had died. But at the time, he could not get the residence
permit he needed to allow him to travel and, in any case, he had no money
to pay for a ticket home. His children, who were two and four when he left,
now, seven years later, had grown up with a photo for a father.

His older son Kalidou was particularly affected, and felt his father's
absence deeply. While his little sister, Aminata, had little memory of her
father, Kalidou, still had clear memories of riding on his Dad's shoulders
and walking to the mosque together to pray. He remembered how proud
he had felt when he wore his gleaming white damask ñetti abdu (a 3 piece
outfit with a pyjama like shirt and pants and a flowing overshirt with open
sides) on *Tabaski* (the feast of the lamb). He held his father's hand as they
walked the sandy road to the local mosque with his little prayer mat under
his arm in the company of the entire community. He always thought of

his father when he heard the call to prayer, because Lamine was a devout Moslem.

Kalidou longed to kick a soccer ball around with his Dad who had been known in his neighborhood for his prowess on the soccer field when he was younger. Kalidou, like many young Africans, had dreams of being a soccer star. He hoped one day his father would be in the grandstands watching him play and cheering. He prayed for his father's return every day and stuck his photo on the wall over his bed with a blue thumbtack. He also prayed for his struggling family, understanding all too well his mother's hardship.

Lamine, too, anesthetized his loneliness and nourished his soul with his photo album and with the new photos he received periodically from his wife, Nafi. He looked forward to the fatter envelopes from home because he knew they could contain new photos. He watched his children grow from afar and could see the pain of a difficult existence without a husband in his wife's face. Her smile always seemed sad.

Nafi, was an enterprising woman and understanding how difficult life was for Lamine in Spain, knew she could not count on him for much financial support. At least not right away. With the little money she had, she began raising chickens in a coop she had built in her courtyard. Each new batch of chicks was purchased at a time that would allow them to mature just before a major holiday. In that way she got the best price for her chickens.

She also had a small table at the front entrance to her compound where she sold peanuts (*gerte caaf*) and candy (*tàngal*) to children and made crispy *akara* (fried bean balls) with hot sauce and sweet *beignets* with coconut every day. Hers were the best in the neighborhood and kids would ask their parents for coins to buy Tantaa (Aunt) Nafy's beignets. She somehow managed to get by.

The village of Yeumbeul where Nafy and Lamine lived is located about 20 kilometres from the center of Dakar at the entrance to the Cap Verde peninsula. Formerly a herders' village, Yeumbeul's population began to swell in the 60's with the influx of people from the interior fleeing the drought. Yeumbeul gradually came to be regarded as a suburb of Dakar. Its population became part of a new, urban proletariat. Unfortunately, many never found the jobs they were seeking and the town is characterized today by high unemployment and frustration among young people looking for work. This explains why so many young men from Yeumbeul and other villages have attempted the dangerous migration by sea from Senegal or overland to Morocco and then by sea to Europe.

Between 2004 and 2009 Senegalese were the second largest African nationality immigrating to Spain after Moroccans, who have a long history of migration to the country. Thousands of young Senegalese left from the coastal cities of Thiaroye, Kayar, Mbour, St. Louis and Kafountine in small, over-crowded boats to try to reach Europe where they hoped to find work. Others, like Lamine went through Mauritania and then crossed the Mediterranean in small boats to reach Italy or Spain. Lamine ended up in Barcelona.

As he attempted to reach the coast of Spain crossing Mauritania to Morocco, Lamine had seen his comrades die in the desert or drown when their flimsy boat had capsized. He had seen specialized crews go out in large, motorized boats to save drowning immigrants. But he had also seen homeless people on the beach in Spain going through the pockets of the drowned corpses looking for anything of value. He thought of the maggots he had seen feeding on the corpses of dead cattle during the last drought. He did not understand why Allah had allowed his friends to die and had spared him. He decided it was a sign that he could not give up, though there were many days of total despair.

On his arrival in Spain, Lamine was received in a Center that had been hastily set up to provide initial assistance to the growing numbers of incoming refugees. There were makeshift dormitories where the immigrants could sleep, get minimal food and clothing, medical care and meet representatives of human rights organizations trying to assist those who qualified for asylum. Some threw their identity cards away and claimed to be from other countries in conflict in order to be granted asylum quickly. Others left the crowded center surreptitiously to go to rural areas where they began picking strawberries, tomatoes or apples until they could find more permanent work.

Many drifted to the larger cities where they imagined it would be easier to find work and the precious contract that was the key to open all doors. It was the contract that allowed the immigrants to have a residence permit which in turn gave them the right to medical care or travel to other countries. This allowed many immigrants to become conveyors importing used cars or shoes or clothing for sale in their countries of origin. Others began working as waiters in bars and restaurants, painting houses, or selling African art objects in the weekly farmers' markets around the country, that resembled the *loumas* they had known in Senegal.

The Spanish government's policy was not to provide care and support to those who did not have the proper papers. Lamine saw other African immigrants die in Spain from poverty, illness and homesickness. Once, he and his friends were called in by the police to help them identify the corpse of an unknown African man whose lifeless body had been found in an alley. He turned out to be someone from Burkina Faso that they did not know. They could tell from the scarification on his face. "Those scars must have scared the white people" Lamine thought silently. He whispered quietly to himself and to God "May the earth rest lightly upon him, and God accept him into his celestial paradise."

As he returned home that night walking through the sad streets of his slum, Lamine had dark thoughts. He wondered, "What would the reaction of my family be if I died in Spain?" Then he thought of his mother and his brother who had died in his absence and he shed some silent tears.

Despite his best efforts, Lamine could not find regular work. He was one of the lucky ones who had made it alive, but his El Dorado quickly turned to hell, living in a crowded room, barely surviving on menial, occasional low paying day jobs, trapped in a ghetto of race and poverty and victim of the daily disdain of the local people and hassles by the police.

Barrio Chino/ South Raval, Barcelona

He lived in a small apartment in a poor neighborhood in Barcelona called South Raval with five other comrades from his Lebou community in Yeumbeul. They shared responsibility for cooking for the group on a rotating basis and helped each other materially and morally to cope with the new environment. This area was located near the port and had the highest levels of poverty in the city. It had also traditionally served as the gateway for new immigrants to the city like Lamine. It had once been known as Barrio Chino or Chinatown.

Southern Raval provided cheap lodging in very poor conditions, in the form of boarding houses, dormitories and subdivided apartments like the one where Lamine lived with his friends. Some of the buildings in South Raval were several centuries old and the existence of slum lodgings in the area could be traced back to the mid 19th century at least.

It was not the change he had hoped for when he left Yeumbeul. Lamine had thought he could escape the grinding poverty and the lack of job opportunities in his country. Instead he found the same desperation but without the means to enjoy the plethora of material things available to those who had everything, and without the social and moral support of his family and friends.

There was, however, the Catalan Association for Senegalese Residents or *Associació Catalana de Residents Senegalesos* (ACRS) where the Senegalese community could go to celebrate Tabaski (Aîd el Kebir) that commemorates Abraham's will to sacrifice his son Ismael to God and Korité (Aîd al-Fitr), that marks the end of the Ramadan month of fasting. They were important moments of communal support that helped to counteract the loneliness of living in another country. They were also moments of almost unbearable nostalgia for home

Lamine worked very hard on learning to speak proper Spanish. Every day he would dress as neatly as possible and go out looking for work in the wealthier communities that surrounded the Raval South slum. On the rare occasions where he could gather some money, he paid his bills and immediately sent most of what remained home to his wife Nafy in Senegal.

He particularly missed his kids and always smiled when he thought of them. He felt guilty not being there to mold them into the adults he wanted them to become. "I wonder what people in the family are teaching them" he thought to himself as he hoped and prayed that his children would become good people in spite of his absence during these critical years.

He especially thought of Kalidou who never stood still and was loved by all. He had *"bayré"* that special magnetism that attracted others to him. To compensate for Kalidou's painful absence, Lamine began kicking the soccer ball around with the young kids in his working class South Raval neighborhood in Barcelona. This gradually evolved into a small, informal "école de foot" or soccer school for young people. He brought the slum kids together with richer kids from the wealthier housing developments near the new Barceló hotel. After some initial clashes, united in their love for soccer, they melded into an inseparable team that would, Lamine hoped, stay in touch for the rest of their lives.

His favorite was 11-year old Carlos who wanted to be an international star. He called himself Rinaldo and was the best player in his group. He reminded Lamine of his Kalidou. He had the same big, dark eyes, the same personality, and worshipped Lamine just like Kalidou did. And like Kalidou he was a charmer who could melt the coldest hearts.

As a good Moslem, Lamine prayed daily, avoided alcohol and only occasionally, when the need for release became too great, resorted to one of the low cost sex workers who walked their neighborhood. The girls liked the Africans because they were muscular, affectionate and generally polite.

After many years of frustration, one of Lamine's roommates was tempted by the lucrative possibility of selling drugs. He was not a criminal, but accepted out of desperation. Lamine tried to convince him not to do it. "*Mar a naan wurul a tax ngay naan pòtit*" he would tell him. (Being thirsty is no reason to drink wash water).

The roommate nevertheless went to see a local *marabout* who had lived in Spain for many years. The *marabout* told the roommate which streets to avoid so as not to be caught up in periodic police dragnets. He also prepared a leather gris-gris for him to wear around his left biceps. Whenever he was in danger of being apprehended by the police, all he had to do was to rotate the gris gris and he would become invisible.

Since the five members of the apartment all shared whatever they had, there followed a period of prosperity. Their housing became a little more comfortable with the addition of a few pieces of used furniture. They had sufficient food and even the possibility of sending money home to Senegal. Lamine tried not to think about where the money was coming from.

Several months later, Lamine and his roommates found themselves in chains at the airport being deported in the most humiliating fashion as local police paraded them like captured animals through the crowds of boarding passengers at his departure gate. Lamine was overcome with shame.

When Nafi saw her husband walk through the doorless cement frame in the wall of their sandy compound in Yeumbeul, she shed the tears she had retained for so long and began sobbing uncontrollably. He was sad, gaunt, unshaven and badly dressed, a far cry from the handsome, ambitious young man who had left for Spain seven years earlier.

He was not the wealthy man that Nafy had imagined he would become. Others had gone to Europe and succeeded. They had built houses for their mothers and wives and returned home wearing fine clothes and bearing gifts for everyone in the family. They fired the imagination and dreams of other young, disenfranchised men in their community who saved up money to pay for passage to Spain in dangerous boats once they reached Morocco. Nafy was caught up in the same illusive mirage and had dreamed of Lamine's return and moving into their big, new home. She had sold the little gold jewelry she possessed to help Lamine raise the three million francs ($6000) he had needed to get to Spain. The family sold the plots of land they owned and contributed the rest.

Family members, friends and acquaintances who learned that Lamine was back filed through the compound all with high expectations of sharing in the wealth that Lamine had brought back from Spain. All left disappointed. None more so than Lamine, who felt covered with shame.

But Lamine was finally home where Nafy could see him and touch him and listen to his soothing voice. Her love and care and the sheer joy of his children to have their father back, helped Lamine to recuperate from his ordeal. At first he could not eat or sleep. Then, he slept a lot and ate regularly and soon was back to a semblance of his old self. He even began to kick the soccer ball around with Kalidou and was impressed with how much his son had grown and what a good football player he had become.

There was also his local mosque where he found much solace and spent hours praying with his *kourous* (prayer beads) for God's intervention and listening to the older men of his community who gathered daily at the "Grand Place" under one of the few remaining Baobab trees. But there was still no work and the situation at home was critical. After a couple of months, Nafy told him the bitter sweet news that she had become pregnant since he returned. She was now often ill with morning sickness that made it more difficult for her to maintain her economic activities.

One terrible night, Kalidou began screaming in pain and complaining of unbearable headaches. He had a high fever and at one point became delirious. They rushed to the local dispensary because they could not afford the transportation and the hospital costs in Dakar. The nurse on duty was young and inexperienced. Kalidou died that night of cerebral malaria and so did the dream of his father cheering him on in the grandstands. Kalidou had been much loved and the family was devastated. Lamine's unshakeable faith in Allah was suddenly in question. "How could God take Kalidou? Had he been preserved where others had fallen only to return home to this excruciating loss?" But his family and community closed ranks around Lamine and Nafy, reminded them that it was God's will (*ndogalu Yàlla*) and, with time, helped them get through this most unspeakable tragedy of parents losing a young child.

Many months later, Lamine was once again downtown looking for work when he saw a youngish, well dressed man, clearly Spanish, trying to purchase vegetables in the Sandaga market in Dakar. With no Wolof and very little French, the man was struggling with the similarities between French and Spanish to try to communicate. But it clearly was not working. Lamine introduced himself in fairly good Spanish and offered to help the man who by now was perspiring profusely with the effort of trying to communicate in languages he did not understand. He welcomed Lamine's assistance and completed his purchases quickly and with a sigh of relief.

His name was Diego. He explained that he had just arrived in Dakar and his wife and son would follow shortly, but for the moment he was on his own. He could not wait until she arrived to handle the management of their home. Buying vegetables was not his strong suit. He invited Lamine for a beer that he declined gracefully, but accepted to sit and have a coke with the gentleman.

He asked Lamine where he had learned to speak Spanish so well. Lamine went on to explain the whole story. He asked him where he had lived in Spain and was delighted to hear that Lamine had been in his own town in Barcelona. When Lamine asked which part of town Diego had lived in, he was surprised to learn that Diego was from the next neighborhood over, near the new Barceló Raval Hotel in a new development with quality shops and private and public housing separated from Lamine's Southern Raval slum by a main thoroughfare. Lamine had been there often looking for work.

Diego explained that he had come to Dakar to open a small hotel that would cater to the many Spanish foreigners and expatriates working in Dakar. It would be a simple, comfortable place with all the conveniences, but unpretentious and reasonably priced and would be called Casa Diego. It would be a kind of home away from home. He would need Senegalese personnel who spoke Spanish and understood their ways and culture to interact with the guests and assist them. Would Lamine be interested?

And so Lamine became Diego's assistant manager with lots of responsibility and a very good salary. His strong work ethic and his honesty quickly confirmed Diego's first, positive impressions. When Lamine accompanied Diego to the airport to pick up his wife and son, he had an unexpected surprise. Holding his mother's hand, a bit daunted by all these Africans running around the airport in a form of organized chaos, was Carlos, Lamine's favorite boy in his football school in Barcelona.

When Carlos saw Lamine, his jaw dropped, he let go of his mother's hand and ran into Lamine's arms calling his name. Tears rolled down Lamine's cheeks. Both parents turned into walking question marks when they saw their son in the arms of this Senegalese man he had no way of knowing. "Papa," explained Carlos excitedly in Spanish, "this is Lamine, my football coach I told you about from Raval in Barcelona!"

That night, Lamine came home to find Nafy in labor. He got a taxi to take her to the maternity ward where she gave birth to a perfect little boy. Once again, Lamine shed tears of joy. The next day, he went to the cemetery in Yeumbeul to pray over Kalidou's little grave. He was convinced that their change of fortune was thanks to Kalidou who had intervened for them in heaven. Even God could not resist his charm.

Author's note:

Parts of this story were inspired by a moving photo exhibit "Présence dans l'Absence" by Dutch artist Judith Quax at the Dutch Ambassador's Residence in Dakar in May 2014. She showed the human face of migration and concentrated on the photos and albums shared with loved ones abroad and with their families at home.

6

OUT OF STEP

◇◇◇

As far back as he could remember, Aliou knew he was different. Growing up in Dakar's Medina in the early 60's, he went to school and kicked the soccer ball around unconvincingly with his friends, but he preferred the company of women.

He liked the way they dressed with the intoxicating fragrance of the little gauze sacs of *gonga* (incense) that they tied to their bra strings and the *jaal jaali* (strings of fragrant beads) they wore around their waists. He liked sitting quietly and unseen in the corner of their room where his sisters were having their hair braided and gossiping. He was particularly amused by his favorite little sister, Maimouna, who always insisted on having colorful beads woven into her corn rows and braids.

Aliou's maternal aunt noticed his proclivities and took him under her wing. She was a respected, powerful woman in the Medina and, like most powerful women had some older, gay men in her entourage. Together they began to groom Aliou for his unusual role in society

Although men are not supposed to cook in Senegal or even enter the kitchen, Aliou was particularly fascinated the artistry of producing delicious, aromatic Senegalese meals. His mother got tired of chasing him out of the kitchen when she was cooking *ceeb u jen* (rice and fish) for the family in a large, three-legged cauldron over a charcoal fire. Over time, he learned to cook and inherited his mother's particular talent. As he got older he was much sought after by the women preparing huge quantities of rice for weddings, funerals or naming ceremonies to help with the cooking.

Over the years, under his Aunt's guidance, he learned the secrets of women. He cooked like his mother. He could braid hair like the best of the *griottes* who did up his sisters' hair in intricate patterns. He learned to crochet and found that it calmed him when he was upset. He also learned to listen and to keep the secrets of the many women who confided in him. These were all skills that when combined provided him with sufficient income to meet his basic needs.

At one point, he began wrapping long scarves around his neck when he went out and developed mildly effeminate mannerisms when he spoke or walked. He gradually became what the Senegalese call a *"goor-jigeen"* (boy-girl)…

Aliou had been a particularly bright student at school and earned the respect of his teachers and his classmates despite his obvious femininity. He was generous with his intelligence and never hesitated to help a friend with homework or tutor someone in French. If he had been in a developed country, he would have been treated as a gifted child and given special instruction. But despite his obvious intelligence, it took him some time to come to terms with his affinity for the company of women and his growing attraction to other men.

For decades if not centuries, the most visible, gay men in Senegal, the more effeminate men and the cross-dressers, had an integral role to play on all levels of Senegalese society. They were advisors to princes, assistants in organizing political campaigns, companions, advisors and helpers to powerful women leaders, organizers of weddings and baptisms, hair braiders, cooks, tailors and most visibly, spectacular dancers in the street *sabaars* or tam tams periodically organized by women's groups in big circles in the neighborhoods or towns. Women came to them to find out ways of making their husbands love them or getting rid of co-wives. They advised women on the latest hair and clothing fashion and on the tailors currently in vogue.

For gay men, the sexual side of things was always discreet as it was between men and women. The British historian Michael Crowder wrote about homosexuality in Saint Louis in the 1950s. He described the discreet meeting places for gay men where they could pick up other men for sexual relations. He noted that the older Moslems advised against these practices. But he found that Africans were very tolerant. They could disapprove of certain behavior on moral grounds without having recourse to physical violence against the behavior they denounced.

But there was always an undercurrent of distaste for homosexuality in Senegal that occasionally found its expression in insults and rock throw-ing by young people against *goor-jigeen* – especially when they left their neighborhoods. The locals were rarely bothered since all the young people had grown up together, everybody knew everybody else and their families, and parents would reprimand their children for annoying the *goor-jigeen* if they did so. Aliou was smart, nice looking, well-liked and enjoyed the protection of his community. Since he had been much loved as a child, he had a contagious self-esteem that made him fun to be with. He did not suffer from the self-loathing frequently found in young gay people around the world.

Aliou gradually discovered that there were other homosexuals who did not look any different from other men their age. They hid their proclivities and only shared them with other gay men whom they met in the course of their pursuit of pleasure. When relations between two men became sexual, the men who appeared less effeminate were often the insertive partners and did not necessarily consider themselves to be homosexuals. The *goor-jigeen* were often the receptive partners. But the roles of gay men could not always be so neatly categorized, with partners using a variety of ways to give each other pleasure and shifting from one role to another as relationships developed and evolved.

In fact, Aliou discovered that there were many more subcategories of homosexuals based on age, status, and type of relationship. He was always amazed at how seemingly timid mice could roar in the bedroom while lions turned into pussycats.

Many married men had mistresses. Some had young, gay men that they visited discreetly while maintaining their roles of husbands and fathers and occupying prestigious positions in Senegalese society. As Aliou matured, he developed an extensive network of both gay and straight friends. His circles of social and sexual activity widened beyond his neighborhood. He soon learned that the lives of many homosexual men were indeed characterized by violence and rejection by their families. He met other *goor-jigeen* who had close relationships with politically and economically powerful women for whom they carried out important errands, social ceremonies and functions and, in turn, received protection. He also learned that not all straight people hated gays and that real friendships were possible. His network of contacts made him influential.

On the chaloupe to Gorée with some friends one Sunday, Aliou met a tall, handsome gay man, and, for the first time, really fell in love. His name was Badou and he was from St. Louis but had spent some time in Europe. He had dark, smooth, ebony-black skin and surprising hazel eyes that gleamed even more brightly in contrast to his complexion. He was one of those beautiful creatures for whom all doors open easily in life. They spent the day together on the island enjoying fresh grilled fish and swimming in the warm ocean.

Aliou loved the way the sunlight shone on Badou's naked, wet chest and the more than promising bulge in his tight, black speedo bathing suit. But most of all, they laughed together — about people they saw, about life in Senegal, about each other. They became fast friends and soon after, became lovers. Aliou knew that this was more important than the crushes he had had on numerous young men over the years. Badou was a soul mate, a potential companion for life. They were compatible.

One of the more frightening aspects of being a *goor-jigeen* in Senegal was the fear of being forced to have sex, by relatives, by friends, by strangers and even by the police. Aliou was clever and avoided situations where he could easily have been raped. He did, however, when he went to new places, occasionally experience verbal abuse, insults and threats and in one or two cases, physical abuse in the form of stone throwing. He rarely spoke of the sexual aspect of his relationships with anyone other than fellow homosexuals and even then, he was selective in his choice of confidants. His partner Badou helped to protect him from abuse when he could. Aliou noted that many of the gay men he knew kept their sexual inclinations and relationships a secret to avoid ostracism, stigmatization, and physical or verbal abuse. Many were bisexual or even married specifically to hide their homosexuality.

Aliou was lucky to have a "husband" but more important to have the support of his neighborhood, of the women in his family and of his gay community mentors. His father and brothers were not particularly pleased that their son/brother was so effeminate. But he was so smart and so sociable that they enjoyed his company and overlooked his sexual ambiguity. In many ways, he somehow escaped many of the negative attitudes and perceptions that form the backdrop for the lives of many gay men in Senegal. Badou was very supportive, but totally discreet and kept a respectful distance from Aliou's family.

Aliou was in his mid-twenties in the early nineties when the AIDS epidemic began decimating the gay community. But for many years, this community was largely ignored by the authorities. Studies around the year 2000 finally revealed the existence of a significant underground gay community in Senegal. Later studies showed high HIV infection rates – ten to twenty times higher than national rates – in this group. The risks of the spread of the virus posed by and to this community became clear. They were finally written into the national strategy.

Many of Aliou's gay friends became mediators in medical facilities and facilitators who organized awareness-raising sessions among gay men. For these young, disenfranchised men, AIDS created not only employment but purpose in life. They became useful in new and different ways. They were helping to stop the spread of AIDS in their country and protecting their community.

Some of the gay men living with HIV had the role of announcing test results to newly diagnosed HIV-infected gay men like themselves. They helped these men regain hope after the shock of the initial announcement of test results, by presenting themselves as examples. "I have had the virus now for three years", they would explain, "but if you take your anti-retrovirals and improve your life style, you can live a nearly normal life for many years to come."

From these friends, Aliou learned about the dangers of unprotected anal intercourse and condoms and how to use them. Gays gradually began to organize themselves in associations in Dakar and throughout the country's 14 regions. Aliou was now pushing forty and did not join an association but nevertheless kept abreast of things happening in the gay community.

Things got much worse in 2008-2009, when a new wave of homophobia swept over Senegal. It was fueled in large part by a religious backlash to a growing visibility of gay men in the tourist centers on Senegal's Petite Côte and a supposed gay marriage covered in a local tabloid accompanied by photos. Aliou and Badou were in a gay club in Saly one night when the police raided. Everyone was having fun just being spontaneous and outrageous in ways they could not do in daily life. The police emptied and closed down the nightclub that was owned and run by a gay French man. Some of their friends were beaten and spent the night in jail, but were released the next day. This was the closest Aliou had come to police brutality and he was angered by the injustice of people being attacked for their sexual orientation when they were doing no harm to anyone.

Thanks to his friends working in the Stop Aids movement, Aliou was able to attend some sessions during the 2008 International conference on AIDS in Africa held in Dakar. That turned out to be an eye-opener for him. He met gay Western and African men and women of all colors, and all nationalities. They were always colorful and united in their demand that their human rights be respected. For the first time he understood the connection between effective AIDS prevention and the inclusion of all sectors of society in the response. He also learned for the first time that five to ten percent of members of all human societies are born with homosexual tendencies. As one gay American friend at the conference explained to him, "We are wired differently from the straight population. We know we are different even before the question of sex arises."

A young woman journalist took a liking to Aliou and sat with him during breaks to drink coffee and talk about his life as a gay man in Senegal. He had always been at ease talking with women. When she told him she wanted to write an article about him for her newspaper, he initially refused. He was, after all, a very private person. But as their friendship grew, he agreed to the article provided names and places were changed, his identity and that of his family and his partner were disguised and there were no photos.

The fact that African gays at the conference came out and actively advocated for their rights elicited a strong backlash. It came from a more extremist version of Islam, and part of a general Moslem radicalization slowly imported over the years from the Middle East by returning koranic teachers and imams. Homosexuality was increasingly perceived as an import from the Western Satan and a tool in the culture wars between Islam and the West. They were shocked and enraged by the conference.

And so began the dark years. For the first time, as he approached fifty, Aliou began to experience real fear and rejection. The changes that ensued included stricter application of the law forbidding acts against nature that had been largely dormant for many years, just like some of the sodomy laws on the books of certain American states. Regular sermons and hostile public discourse and media expressing the ambient homophobia all led to harsher treatment and greater exclusion of gay people. It made gay bashing fashionable, acceptable and even proof of being a good Moslem.

Aliou tried to dress more conservatively and even tried to change the way he walked, to avoid having stones thrown at him in neighborhoods where he was not known. His relationship of 23 years did not survive the new pressures in the community. Badou could no longer live in an environment that defined him daily as nothing more than a gay man. He could not stand the constant persecution anymore and finally decided to seek asylum in the Netherlands. He begged Aliou to come with him, but Aliou did not want to leave his country. He could not imagine himself living in Europe, even with Badou at his side. They reluctantly decided to part company leaving Aliou, who was nearing fifty, exposed and alone for the first time in many years. It took Aliou a long time to recover from this unexpected separation.

A once relatively tolerant and compassionate Senegal had begun to fall under the influence of the more conservative Moslems who were using the fight against homosexuality as their battle cry. Their strict interpretation of Islam was in the ascendance and no one wanted to be seen publicly as a bad Moslem. They created a sort of Senegalese schizophrenia. On the one hand the Senegalese based their lives on fundamental cultural values of tolerance and understanding and, on the other, they believed in adherence to stricter Moslem or Christian religious values. By emphasizing religious orthodoxy, the extremists were able to push a significant segment of Senegal's 85% to 95% Moslem majority into a frenzy of anti-homosexual activity.

Under the leadership of an Islamic NGO, the fundamentalists had several major successes over that two-year period. They sent delegations to all the heads of Senegal's powerful Moslem Sufi brotherhoods where they succeeded in creating fear and panic. They told stories of obscure Western gay lobbies advocating for gay marriage and the rights of a growing horde of gay men in Senegal who would soon trample on traditional Moslem values. They spoke of young people being "recruited" into homosexual prostitution as an alternative to unemployment. They threw the issue of pedophilia into the mix to make sure that no right-minded person would refuse to adhere to their cause.

They succeeded in convincing leaders of Senegal's brotherhoods to deliver coordinated, repeated sermons against homosexuality and homosexuals every Friday in Mosques across the country. Aliou felt increasingly ashamed and alienated when he heard imams speaking out against homosexuality. He was a practicing Moslem. He had not felt he had done anything wrong. He was just being who he was and loving the men he loved. Now, for the first time in his life, he really wanted to hide.

The anonymous article about him finally came out in Senegal's internet newspapers and on the front page of one of Senegal's dailies. It turned out to be one of the better-written, more sensitive articles on gay men that had come out in the Senegalese media and flew off the newsstands. The Senegalese have an insatiable appetite for stories about homosexuality. As expected, there were many negative reactions. But what was most surprising and what pleased Aliou, was the large number of positive, sympathetic responses. Readers who wrote letters to the editor signing their names under the disguise of initials or pseudonyms were released from social pressures and freed to express a more tolerant 'live and let live' attitude. It was the beginning of a timid, new, more open social dialogue that would continue for years to come.

Aliou was now older and alone. Many gay men including several of his friends had died. Others, like Badou, had gone into hiding or exile, making it difficult for medical authorities to continue their work with these communities on AIDS prevention and care. After the homophobic events in 2009, prevention and care activities for this community were virtually

suspended for over nine months. This placed the entire Senegalese population, including Aliou, at greater risk of HIV.

When the extremists placed the issue of homosexuality in the con-
text of Western aggression against Moslem values, Aliou felt as though he
had been stabbed in the heart. The extremists rejected international norms
that included a call for respect of the rights of sexual minorities signed
by Senegal such as the Universal Charter of Human Rights (1948), the
International Covenant on Civil and Political Rights (1966), the African
Charter on Human and People's Rights of people (CADHOP – Gambia
1981) to mention a few.

For the extremists, homosexuals had no rights. For them, the signing
of these documents was proof that their leaders had sold out to the West.
For a brief moment, Aliou felt like a traitor for being gay. But in school, he
had learned the value and importance of these treaties and he believed in
the Universal Charter of Human Rights. He knew that everyone should be
protected under these declarations, including gay men. He began to feel
that he was being excluded from his own society. Finally, after much soul
searching, he concluded that it was his country that was out of step with
the modern world.

The cultural status of the "*goor-jigeen*" had developed over time and
was both inclusive and consistent with the optimal use of their particular
skills and sensitivities as contributing members to the functioning of society. It also coincided with Senegalese values of *yermande* (compassion),
sutura (respecting the private lives and peccadillos of others), and *kersa*,
(considering the feelings of others and avoiding doing or saying things
that shock or offend), among others. The new wave of homophobia began
destroying this intricate, inclusive social architecture that had ensured
greater equity and equilibrium for hundreds of years. The extremists were
trampling upon millennial values that have kept this culture going for
decades despite the challenges of poverty, drought, colonialism and war.
Aliou still found his place in his community and in the homes of certain

friends where he was always welcome, but the world where he could be who he was and feel secure was clearly shrinking.

With this powerful wave of religious sentiment behind them, the NGO succeeded in creating a new, imaginary threat – an alleged agreement between the Senegalese and US Presidents to repeal the law against homosexuality in Senegal in order to comply with terms for massive financial aid.

Government figures including the Prime Minister and Minister of Justice were all human rights activists prior to entering the government. But early in his presidency, the new Senegalese leader was challenged by the religious right to state his position on changing the law on unnatural acts. The political storm created forced the new, liberal-minded president of Senegal to declare that the decriminalization of homosexuality and gay marriage would never occur under his regime. His country was not ready. He and his Ministers became virtual hostages of the extremists in order to preserve their political careers. This created a sort of omerta around the issue of homosexuality that set back progress in the liberalization of attitudes and laws concerning LGBTI in Senegal.

In May of 2013, the Islamic NGO created an observatory roughly translated as "refuge of virtue" to watch over and defend "cultural and religious values." They claimed to wish to create a powerful front against mental and cultural alienation, the decline of morality, and the systematic sacrifice of the mental and moral equilibrium of their children on the altar of profit and easy gain. "From now on," they announced, "each time that our culture or our religion are attacked, it will not only be our NGO leading the battle but an alliance of a dozen social movements." The thought police was in place.

Aliou listened, watched and analyzed the situation. Rather than being a refuge of virtue, he felt that this new Observatory could be a wedge for the further introduction of massive violations of human rights, particularly the right to privacy and other civil liberties in the name of religious correctness. Clearly, the observatory needed to be observed…

Unlike the heads of the traditional Sufi Moslem brotherhoods in Senegal who may influence government decisions but do not particularly wish to govern, the leader of the religious wing of the Islamist NGO movement was also an ambitious politician. Aliou wondered how much of his motivation was to consolidate and expand his political power base using fear and emotionally charged issues to advance his political career. Years earlier, the same extremists had scapegoated women's liberation and modernization of the laws regulating the family. Now it was the turn of the homosexuals to be blamed for all of societies ills

But Aliou remembered the biblical quote "Judgement is mine sayeth the Lord." He believed that gay people should not be judged by other members of their society. If they had really sinned, which he strongly doubted, this was between them and God. Islam, that provides the ultimate guidelines for the many Moslems in Senegal, had also taught Aliou that speaking evil of others was a serious sin. Allah compared the sin of calumny to the person who eats the flesh of his dead brother. In his farewell speech, the prophet said: "Those of you who have believed with your tongues and not with your hearts, do not speak badly of Moslems or try to identify their shortcomings. Those who search for the shortcomings of others will have their own shortcomings revealed by God, even within their own households." What of those who accused or persecuted people based on their perceived sexual orientation?

An aging Aliou lived on sweet memories. There were no more casual relationships with handsome young men. Though he and his one true love had lost contact over the years, Badou was often in his thoughts and dreams. He had gradually been transformed into a quiet activist in his declining years. He was not a public speaker, but he was very effective in one on one discussions with friends and acquaintances. His ability to listen and his respect for the secrets of those who confided in him made him a trusted "aunt" for his community. Each day, both young and older gay men came to sit with him and talk as he crocheted and listened to them intently, occasionally offering an insight or a suggestion.

Like a growing number of Senegalese, Aliou was terribly uncomfortable with the new trends in the practice of Islam in his country and equally uncomfortable with the institutionalized persecution of a segment of Senegalese society. The silence in government circles became deafening. There was a need for people to begin questioning their own prejudice and that of their society and speaking out. He was convinced that they could search for solutions in their rich cultural heritage. Aliou hoped that the creation of the Observatory, like the publication of the article about him years before, would be another trigger for the many more liberal-minded Senegalese from all walks of like who were viscerally uncomfortable with the increasing dominance of a more conservative form of Islam, to begin to react publicly despite their fear of being labeled as "bad Moslems".

Aliou was pleased that he had been able to affect the lives of a certain number of people with his quiet militancy, but he probably never realized that he had profoundly touched the life of a young woman named Coumba. She was interviewed recently on a local radio program about her own process of becoming aware of her prejudice against gay people:

"I remember being very young. I am not sure what age I was. But I used to go to my Aunt's place and she had friends. She had lots of friends. And among them she had some friends who were gay. There was one of them whose name was Aliou who has since passed away. There were actually three gay men in my Aunt's entourage and all have passed away... "

"You know how here, all the time, people, children when you say hello you always grab somebody's hand and shake it. Seriously, I really don't know where or how I got this idea, but when I was at my Aunt's house and realized or heard that Aliou was gay, I decided I was not going to shake his hand anymore. So I told my Mom in Wolof *"Duma ko nuyu"* - I am not going to greet him!" And she said "Why?" "Why wouldn't you shake his hand?" And I answered "Because he is a *goor jigeen*!" And she said "but why?" And I whispered "If you shake his hand, you go to hell when you die!" And as a child, I really believed that. I still can't tell you who told me that or where I heard it. Maybe it was transmitted to me by my little girl-friends during the children's games that we played...But I just knew that if I shook his hand, when I died I would go to hell."

"So my Mom who is some kind of [laughter] some kind of, I don't know, free spirit, she said, 'I don't think so, Coumba' "When you come here and you shake other people's hands, and you don't shake Tonton Aliou's hand, don't you think he will feel sad or bad about it? And he's a human being, one of God's creations...." almost making me feel like okay, wouldn't that take you to hell more quickly than anything else? And so, yeah, I ended up definitely continuing to go to my Aunt's house and shaking Tonton Aliou's hand, But still today I remember the prejudice and, uh, just not only the fear of going to hell, because I don't even know what is in hell. But just that not shaking his hand is wrong."

"As I got to know Tonton Aliou better over the years I found him to be very nice, very peaceful. He used to come to our house, too, and sit and talk quietly crocheting with my mother, which is something mainly women do, while I was having my hair braided."

"And my mother later told me how he took care of his Mom in the Medina when she was dying. I think he was an only child or maybe not, maybe he had other brothers and sisters, but he was the person who was there at his Mom's side, taking care of her. And my mother told me that when Aliou's Mom died, he did everything. With quiet tears streaming down his face, he took care of his mother's lifeless body, lighting incense, dressing her, making everything nice before calling other people in. And when I heard that I thought 'Tonton Aliou was a great person.' It doesn't matter that people say he was gay. I could just feel fundamentally that he was a good person."

"This is one of the stories that formed me. So I asked myself, how do we break from prejudice? What do we do? And I think we need to go back to the beginning of it, to the source of it. Like how do people know these things that they are saying about gay people, that they are wrong, that they are this or that? Like anybody who tells you that, you know, we need to ask them how do they know it? Like who do they know who the gay person was mean to, or did this or that to them? Or where did they find all that — and I think that could definitely help to change people's perceptions."

"I think these experiences are what really shaped me and changed my mindset, and my prejudice. I was just trying to explain, you know, when people ask me what makes me so open— me, and not somebody else. I think it is really the experience of being close to people and knowing them in other ways rather than just hearing things and believing them and just projecting what you hear on other people."

Coumba was right about a lot of things. She was correct about Aliou's death. He had died quietly around midnight one night in his family home in the Medina in the same bed where he had prepared his mother for burial. His crochet needles and thread were at his side next to his copy of the Koran. It seemed as though he had known he was dying and had straightened everything up, put on his spotless, white khaftan, wrapped his prayer beads around his wrist, and lied down quietly to return to Allah.

His body was taken to the room that served as a morgue in the old, local mosque on Rue Onze that had been the center of the community since before independence. A team of men washed his slender body, placed cotton in all his orifices and dressed him in a loincloth. They tied his arms crossed across his chest and his legs around the ankles and wrapped him in percale. They lit incense and sprinkled eau de cologne on the percale and then invited those who wanted to view the body to file around the table in the morgue before taking him out for burial.

All the men of the neighborhood came to the courtyard of the mosque and prayed as one, over Aliou's body, shoulder to shoulder, to ask Allah to forgive him and have mercy on him as they would do for any deceased person from their community. Aliou's body was carried to a waiting black panel truck with a decorative serrated border around the roof that served as a hearse. Many of the men accompanied the body to the cemetery where Aliou was lowered into the waiting grave in the hands of his friends and neighbors and laid on his side facing Mecca.

This was unlike the scenes in some other places in Senegal where gays were refused burial in the local cemetery by angry crowds or even had their corpses exhumed and dragged through the streets. Here the community had mobilized. Back on Rue Treize, they had set up chairs and a tent that blocked traffic. After the burial, hundreds of people from the neighborhood and elsewhere whose lives Aliou had touched, gradually joined the mourners to present their condolences to his sisters and brothers and their families. There were many testimonials, all of them respectful, loving and grateful. At one point, when Aliou's favorite younger sister, Maimouna, looked up through her tears, she thought she saw a tall, dark man with greying hair and gleaming hazel eyes standing silently and watching from a corner of the tent…

7
TEST OF TIME

◇◇

June 2003: A lone podium in the middle of the field faced an expanse of tents that protected about 300 guests from the African sun. The Peace Corps Director who was also a former Senegal volunteer, had invited me to speak at the swearing in ceremony of the new Peace Corps Volunteers in Senegal. It was a special day because it was also the 40th anniversary of Peace Corps in Senegal. The first volunteers had arrived in 1963. I was in the third group that came in 1965 and had been in Senegal ever since. So the Director asked me, as the "dean" of former volunteers, to speak in the name of the nearly 3000 volunteers who have served in Senegal over the past forty years. It was a challenge, an honor and an exercise in retrospection, synthesis and completion.

The ceremony took place at the site of the proposed new, as yet unbuilt, Ambassador's Residence in a large open field overlooking the sea, lovingly know as Ebbets Field in the American community. That had particular significance for me because I had grown up in Brooklyn and, like everyone else where I grew up, was a fervent Dodger's fan until they betrayed us and moved to Los Angeles. It was a typically sunny, early June day with a pleasant breeze blowing off the Atlantic. The more humid rainy season or "*hivernage*" was still a couple of weeks away.

To mark the special day, Peace Corps had organized a buffet and set up an orchestra playing Senegalese music. The guests included the new volunteers to be sworn in and those ending their two year service, the host families that had housed the new volunteers during their recently completed training program, the training and administrative staff of Peace Corps Senegal and their training center, and guests from the development community, including many former Peace Corps Volunteers. In the front row under the tents, high-level representatives of the Senegalese government sat next to the US Ambassador, who was himself a Returned Peace Corps Volunteer who had served in Burkina Faso.

I was one of several speakers, including the Ambassador, the Peace Corps Director, a member of the training staff and a Senegalese woman who had not only housed several generations of Volunteers but had herself benefited from awareness-raising and income-generating activities initiated by Peace Corps. The highlight of these ceremonies is always the speeches delivered in several national languages by the incoming volunteers who have just completed their training. They spoke with surprising fluency after only eight weeks of study, in several of Senegal's national languages to the delight of all present. Peace Corps is known for its effectiveness in teaching national languages.

There are lots of funny stories about how the Senegalese reacted to the relatively recent phenomenon of Americans who learn to speak their language fairly fluently. The typical reaction was a look of surprise, and with hand over the mouth, the Senegalese would declare: *Laay Laa tubaab bi deggne olof*" (Oh my God, this white person speaks wolof!"

One volunteer tells the story of hailing a taxi around midnight and announcing his destination in Wolof. The taxi driver turned around and looked at him with a terrified expression and then floored the gas pedal because he thought he had picked up a *djinn* (spirit) since he had never seen a white person who spoke Wolof.

My favorite is the story told by my friend Riall Nolan who went on to become a prominent professor of anthropology. He tells of how in the late sixties, months after settling into Etiolo, way out in South Eastern corner of Senegal and learning to speak the little-studied language of the Bassari fairy fluently, he decided to hike over the ridge to visit some of the surrounding villages several kilometers away that he had not yet seen. He was gifted for languages and his reputation had spread.

Walking was the only means of transportation in this rocky, mountainous zone. During this particular trek he came across an isolated compound, which is often the way the Bassari live. He saw a very old woman sitting alone on a log that had been placed in front of her hut to serve as a bench. Following local custom, Riall sat way over on the other end of the log with his back turned to the woman. They gradually exchanged greetings in Bassari quietly as was the custom, and chatted for a while without facing each other.

Then a little girl came out of the hut and stood quietly for a moment evaluating the situation. Finally she said: "Grandmother, do you know you are speaking to a white man? "

The old lady turned around and Riall saw that she was blind. \"So you speak our language? " The old woman asked rhetorically.

"Yes" said Riall modestly. " I am learning."

The old woman responded: "You know, There's another toubab in the next valley over the ridge who also speaks our language. His name is Nolan, but he speaks it better than you do."

As I spoke to the audience, I could hear my amplified words echoing across the field. I said that I was going to try to talk about the common threads, the shared experiences or lessons learned by all volunteers who had served in Senegal over the past forty years, not an easy task. I wanted to accurately represent the experience so that volunteers would recognize themselves in what I was describing. The other goal was to help the many guests in the audience to better understand the significance of volunteer service for the young (and not so young) volunteers who come here.

Starting from the three Peace Corps goals (roughly summarized: development assistance, better understanding of Americans by host country people, better understanding of host country by Americans), I discussed the obvious benefits to Volunteers of learning through doing, especially in a different cultural setting.

The volunteer has an impact on local development in small, lasting ways that gradually become part of community life. Years later, the younger people in the village would assume that things have always been that way until an older member of the community explains the story of Aminata Sene or Ibrahima Ndiaye, the American volunteer whose real name has long vanished from their memories but whose local name has remained. They explain how s/he had helped introduce market gardening, sunk a bore-hole well, built a maternity clinic, planted mango trees or taught English, leaving behind a small but significant change in the quality of life.

Returned volunteers can also be important resources to their own families, communities and country. I asked the former volunteers present in the audience to stand. The point was made when about thirty people rose to the ringing applause of the guests. They included the American Ambassador himself, various USAID and Embassy officials, heads of NGOs and project directors and administrators.

But for those who have never had the Peace Corps experience, it was important to insist on the less obvious, but perhaps more profound and lasting effect on the Volunteer. It was the experience of being integrated into another culture with warmth and support from host families. When Volunteers speak of their sister, brother or mother it is often impossible to know whether they are referring to their family in the US or to their host family in Senegal!

Senegalese "mothers" protect these Volunteers because they are "someone's child." They hope that if their children ever find themselves overseas without the support of friends and the family network, that people will treat them kindly and protect them from the total poverty and discouragement that can happen when one is alone and broke in a foreign country. They call it "*tumeranké.*" They feel that if they treat "someone's child" with kindness, that they will be rewarded by having their child treated with kindness as well and avoid "*tumeranké.*" A sort cosmic repayment for good deeds or a Senegalese version of karma…

Peace Corps Volunteers in Senegal, no matter what their program or the years during which they served, have all participated in the life of a culture that reminded them daily about the importance of people in responding to the needs and helping to solve the problems of others. All of them have learned the meaning of the much-repeated Wolof proverb "*Nit, nit ay garabam.*" Roughly translated it means, "Man is the remedy for Man." They say "You are born into the hands of other people, and you are carried to your final resting place in the hands of others." It is a philosophy based on the idea that any problem we may encounter as human beings can be resolved by other people - not necessarily by individual effort, but by our web of interpersonal relations.

Well-managed inter-cultural experiences can be profound and enduring for those who share this adventure. It can create long lasting links between people around the world. I recorded an interview with one volunteer who returned to Senegal for a visit almost thirty years after his service. He swore to me that a day did not go by when he did not mention Senegal or think of the years he had spent in his village. He remembered the sound of the pre-dawn call of the muezzin to prayer and the scent of *curaay* (incense) that permeated Senegalese homes. Sometimes a Senegalese song or a phrase in Wolof or Pulaar would pop into his head, even though his fluency in the local languages had long since faded with disuse. But most of all, he remembered his Senegalese family and went to visit the village where he had served while he was here. He began to cry as he told me that when he got to his village he learned that his Senegalese father, the village chief, had died several years ago. "Turn that thing off," he said.

In July 2003, a young Senegalese Catholic colleague from a local NGO provided me with another lesson on the enduring nature of the links established between Peace Corps volunteers and the people they work with in their host countries. He called me aside to ask for a favor. "I know you were a Peace Corps volunteer many years ago," he said. "Did you happen to know a Volunteer named Jerry Grondin?"

"Yes," I said, "I remember that name and sort of remember Jerry as well."

"Well," explained my young colleague, "Jerry was a track and field trainer in 1974-75 and also worked in an orphanage. He trained my uncle Robert who is today [almost thirty years later] a senior official at the Direction of Territorial Administration. My uncle was a member of Senegal's 1974 national high jump team that Jerry trained. Jerry found a two-year sports scholarship for my uncle in Chicago but my aunt [Robert's mother] felt he was too young and did not let him go. Jerry returned to the States in 1975 and my uncle would really like to get back in touch with him..."

Many former volunteers have another type of impact. They communicate their love of Senegal and the value of their experience to their families and friends who have never been here. This is part of the third goal of Peace Corps: "better understanding of the host country by Americans.". Bringing the experience home...

Ginny Neely, had worked in a social center program in the 70's. When Ginny left Senegal after two years of service, she met and married a returned volunteer from India. They had two children, a son and a daughter. Ginny always told her children and their friends magical stories about her time as a volunteer in Tivaouane. The kids were surrounded with African and Indian artifacts and Peace Corps stories from both their parents. Ginny, in particular, transmitted her love for the Senegalese people and her lasting gratitude for the love they had given her. One of her daughter's friends subsequently joined Peace Corps and went to Paraguay as a result of Ginnys stories..

Tragically, Ginny died young, in her late forties leaving a gaping hole in the lives of her family. She was sorely missed. Several years later, her then17-year-old daughter Margot told her father that she wanted to travel to Senegal to try to better understand why this experience had been so important to her mother Ginny. She was looking for a way to somehow continue connecting with her deceased mother. She wanted to visit the town where her mother had served as a Volunteer. Her father realized how important this trip was for Margot, and though he was concerned about his young daughter traveling alone to Africa, he trusted her maturity. He made a few calls to people who might be able to facilitate his daughter's journey. My partner and I were among those contacted. I had known Ginny when she had been a volunteer 30 years earlier. We agreed to do whatever we could to help.

Margot arrived in Senegal. With a little help from us and a lot of determination on her part, she managed to get to the town of Tivaouane in a seven place bush taxi. Rail transport had been suspended in most of Senegal and the railway station in the center of Tivaouane was no longer in use.

This town is in the Region of Thies. It was part of the Wolof kingdom of Cayor, and was at one time its capital. It was first described to Europeans in the 15th century by Venitian explorer Luigi Cada-Mosto. In 1904, it was the fifth largest city in Senegal after Saint Louis, Dakar, Rufisque and Gorée.

More important, Tivaouane is the capital of the Tijaniya Sufi brotherhood, the largest in Senegal. It is known for two Senegalese historic monuments: the mausoleum of El-Hadji Malick Sy and the mosque of Serigne Babacar Sy. Each week, followers come to visit the tombs of these religious leaders. Literally hundreds of thousands of visitors flock each year to Tivaouane to celebrate the birth of the prophet Muhammed in a festival called the Maouloud (or *Gamou*, in Wolof).

But Margot was not really interested in the sights of Tivaouane. She had a mission and very little time. She was armed with pictures of her mother and went directly to the neighborhood where she knew her mother had lived. She learned some basic Wolof greetings, and with the help of a local interpreter, began asking people of her mother's age if they had known Ginny Neely. She showed them the pictures and told them what she knew about her mother's work with Peace Corps in Senegal. Most Senegalese knew *"les volontaires américains"* or as many pronounce it "Peace Corpse" with no intention of disrespect. To Margot's satisfaction, she gradually met people who had known and worked with her mother as a Volunteer. But she was yet to understand the extent of what she had discovered.

Two of the women still had photos of her mother that they had saved. They were a bit faded and worn from time and handling but were clearly important souvenirs for their owners. In the pictures, Margot saw a younger and very happy version of her Mom. She could feel the excitement of the Peace Corps adventure through the photo. In a couple of pictures, she thought she was looking at herself. The women spoke warmly of her mother and the good work she had done at the social center to provide skills training for members of women's groups so that they could develop income-generating activities. Margot was proud that her mother was remembered so warmly by women who could not speak English and barely spoke French.

But her discoveries were not yet complete. A third woman's eyes filled with tears when she learned that her old friend Ginny had passed away and realized that she was talking to Ginny's daughter. She fondly pressed Margot's upper arm repeating the word *"massa, massa doom"* a wolof expression used to relieve pain in others. "Take heart, my child, take heart."

Her name was Fatou. She noted Margot's resemblance to her mother. She invited Margot into her little home and began serving Senegalese tea, *ataaya*, telling Margot about moments shared with her mother, as she brewed the three successive little glasses. Margot instinctively knew that this woman had been very close to her mother.

After a while, the woman pulled out an old, rusted metal box from under her bed where she kept memorabilia. She pulled out an envelope yellowed around the edges by time and handed it to Margot. As she pulled out the card it contained, Margot realized that this woman had saved the wedding invitation that Ginny had sent her 31 years before. Her mother had wanted to share this important passage in her life with her old Senegalese friend. "Of course, she knew that the woman could not come to the wedding," Margot thought to herself. But she understood that her mother had wanted Fatou to be part of this significant passage in her life even if she could never attend. Margot felt the intensity of a friendship that had transformed an old wedding invitation into a precious symbol carefully preserved. She understood the complicity that had developed between these two women from different cultures.

But there remained a fourth surprise on the next to the last day of Margot's trip. A woman named Arame came to see her, accompanied by her daughter. The Senegalese have an extremely effective word of mouth communication system that puts internet to shame! The woman had learned from her friend that Ginny's daughter was in town. Margot estimated her to be about 45 but had already discovered that the Senegalese men and women she met were often older than they appeared.

She introduced herself and explained that she had been one of Ginny's assistants at the social center. Arame presented her condolences to Margot even though her Mom had been dead for over four years. Margot was particularly fascinated by this woman. She had surprising almond-shaped, almost oriental eyes, an engaging smile and beautiful skin that set off perfect white teeth. She was simply dressed in a patterned cotton *boubou* with an unpretentious matching head tie hiding her hair. She was a simple woman, obviously not very well to do but she exuded poise and confidence.

Then came the final surprise of Margot's mission. Arame introduced her daughter who was a younger version of her mother, with the same almond-shaped eyes. She said her name was "Neely" and explained that she had given Ginny's last name "Neely" as a first name to this daughter. Her mother's name had been pronounced daily in Arame's house for 25 years! Her memory was alive and well in Tivaouane.

It was evening and the gentle call to prayer of the mosque was hypnotic. Back in the room of her funky hotel, Margot was now seeing what her mother had seen and hearing what her mother had heard. She was beginning to understand the relationships that her mother had managed to weave with these extraordinary women from a totally different culture. She realized how deep and lasting the relationships were and finally understood why they had been so important to her mom.

While Margot was in Tivaouane, two of the women took her to the house where her mother had lived as a volunteer. It was a simple three-room banco house with a corrugated tin roof. Margot imagined the noise it must have made when it rained. She pictured her mother sitting with her roommate reading by candlelight in the evenings. Her mother had told her that they did not have electricity. But things had obviously changed.

A young Senegalese family now occupied the house and, though they had not known her mother, they allowed Margot to visit their home once she explained that her defunct mother had lived there many years ago. They now had electricity and running water, though the house both indoors and outdoors was badly in need of a coat of paint. The children's hand prints were visible on most of the walls and the linoleum covering the concrete floor was cracked in places. Everyone was very gracious and the curious kids gradually warmed up to the *toubab* stranger and approached diffidently to greet her and touch her unusual skin. They seemed like a happy family and Margot found the children to be neat, well-dressed and polite.

They invited her to stay for dinner but she declined politely. She wanted to stay longer but had to get back to Dakar to catch her plane so that she could be back in the US in time for school. Before Margot left the house, she picked up a few small stones from the gravel surrounding the house and gently placed them in her bag.

On her return to North Carolina, she sat with her father and brother for several hours recounting every detail of her time in Senegal. There were tears. There were smiles and laughter. She showed them pictures of the people she had met and the places she had visited. Then she leaned over and whispered into her father's ear. He smiled and nodded his head.

The next day, Margot and her father and brother visited the cemetery where her mother was buried. When they arrived at her mother's plot, they quietly removed the weeds that had grown up around the grave. Margot slowly reached into her bag and respectfully placed the small stones she had carried back from her mother's house in Tivaouane, one by one, on Ginny's tombstone.

8

KOLERE LOOKS
TO THE PAST

You would not expect a guy named Rudy Gomis to be from Africa. Maybe Portugal or Brazil but not Africa! But between the Portuguese past of his native Casamance Region of Senegal which accounted for the Gomis, and a father who had been a Catholic veteran of Dien Bien Phu, which explains the Rodolphe, we were left with a teacher trainee named Rudy Gomis who also became a lead vocalist in Senegal's legendary Baobab Orchestra.

Rudy was a promising participant in our language teacher-training program. He had energy and humor and was a born actor. He was already involved in music and had street smarts and a keen understanding of human nature. He quickly mastered the oral participatory techniques we were using based on the teachings of Dartmouth Professor John Rassias. For many years that followed, Rudy taught French and African languages for our American Study Abroad students, foreign aid workers and independent learners from countries all over the world.

He was truly an excellent, challenging teacher. He put real pressure on his students but provided loving support at the same time. Linguistic tough love. And his students loved him for it. The combination of his effectiveness as a teacher and his star quality as one of Senegal's best known singers made him one of the most popular teachers at our center. Even out of class, he always found time for his students.

Rudy made his first trip to the US in the late seventies to visit an American girlfriend and meet her upper class African American family. There was a possibility of marriage in the air and he was received with great warmth and hospitality. But he quickly became aware that the cultural gap between him and his American hosts would be too great to bridge were he to marry their daughter. He was offended by some of the African American preconceptions of a primitive Africa. At the same time, he was overwhelmed by the immense wealth of America and those who lived there, which he found to be obscene given the extreme poverty in the rest of the world.

Rudy Gomis

One of Rudy's main challenges in the family was a large grey Siamese house cat named Caesar. Caesar did not like Rudy from the moment he entered the house. But the relationship reached crisis proportion one weekend when the family had to go away for an overnight, and Rudy was left alone in the house with instructions on how to feed and take care of Caesar. The cat had his own little fridge in which the family kept Caesar's food, already divided into daily portions. All Rudy had to do was to unwrap one portion at a time and feed Caesar at the appropriate moments.

The first evening, Caesar sat himself down in front of the fridge indicating to Rudy that is was time for dinner. Caesar was not one of those obsequious cats who would wind themselves around the legs of their owners, purring or meowing to let them know they wanted something. Caesar knew his rights and simply placed himself in the appropriate position in front of his fridge waiting to receive his due.

When Rudy opened the fridge and unwrapped a package of Caesar's dinner, he discovered it was first grade beef liver. Given the fact that he was not used to having house pets and was morally opposed to feeding good quality liver to cats, and the fact that he loved liver brochettes, he took a large slice and threw it into a frying pan with some cumin, onions and a little olive oil for his own dinner and gave Caesar the remaining liver in the package. Caesar gobbled down his dinner quickly and then sat right down in front of Rudy glaring at him as he ate a portion of Caesar's liver. Rudy shooed him away but Caesar did not move. He just sat and stared until Rudy had finished and then hissed at him when Rudy stood up, turned his back and walked away in a huff. From then on, every time Caesar saw Rudy, he hissed.

The next day, when the family returned, they were all sitting in the living room talking about their overnight, when Caesar walked by and hissed at Rudy.

"What did you to Caesar, Rudy?" his girlfriend's father asked.

"I ate a piece of his liver!"

"Oh, no wonder he's so angry. He doesn't like people messing with his food!"

After a couple of weeks, when Rudy had concluded that he did not want to make his life in the US, he announced to his friends that he had decided to go back to DC and then on to Dakar. They were surprised because it was the dream of every young Senegalese man to get to the States. His girlfriend was disappointed and tried everything to convince him to stay but he was adamant.

So when the day came for him to take the bus to DC, his friends packed him a travel lunch before he left Chicago. On the bus, when Rudy got hungry, he began to unwrap his sandwich. But he was uncomfortable. Senegalese always share food. They have been taught to share since they were children. An adult seeing a child walking around eating bread or fruit or candy will invariably say: "*Mai ma*" – give me some – so that the act of sharing becomes ingrained. Those children grow up to be uncomfortable eating alone without inviting the people around them to join.

Riding on the bus between Chicago and DC, as evening fell, and Rudy took out the sandwich that had been lovingly prepared for him for the trip, he turned and offered to share it with the stranger sitting next to him. The man was surprised and initially refused but finally accepted on Rudy's insistence. The man was obviously hungry and enjoyed the gift of unexpected sustenance.

Rudy was struck by the fact that at the next rest stop, the man rushed to get off the bus to buy a pack of cigarettes that he offered to Rudy on his return. He could sense that the man had been uneasy with the idea of owing something to the stranger next to him without being able to do something in return. Only when Rudy accepted the cigarettes did the man seem to feel that equilibrium had been reestablished.

"American *kolere*" mused Rudy as he fell into a light sleep, smiling to himself.

Kolere (pronounced Ko-lair-ray) was one of those key wolof values that he regularly explained to his foreign students. He explained to them that it encompasses loyalty, gratitude, appreciation, obligation and recognition. It remembers and acknowledges the good that people have done for you in the past and values the ties that have been created by those good deeds. They say that "kolere faces backwards", *[kolere ginaaw ley fete];* it looks back to the past and is based on not forgetting and on maintaining the connections that have been created during past social interactions. It is another element in the glue that holds together the intricate Senegalese social architecture.

Ideally, it is a noble value that can even pass from one generation to the next. On Tabaski, the feast of the lamb, for example, which commemorates Abraham's willingness to sacrifice his son Ishmael, a sheep is sacrificed in each Moslem home. The meat is distributed to family and friends. A daughter whose mother is deceased may send a leg of lamb to a person who was kind to her mother when she lived, but has no blood relationship with the family. For centuries, on the feast of the sacrifice, known as Eid-al-Adha in Arabic, Moslems have sent portions of freshly sacrificed lamb to Christian friends. The Christians, in turn, have for hundreds of years, been sending buckets of *ngelaax* (a millet and peanut porridge) to their Moslem friends in Senegal around the Easter holidays.

Rudy enjoyed explaining how, with the help of strong oral history, some of these *kolere* relationships can become familial obligations and can be passed from one generation to another. Families not related biologically can become bound together over time in a preferential relationship that the great grandchildren may not fully understand. Nevertheless, they take this relationship as a given and continue to nourish it, having been inculcated with a sense of duty based on *kolere*. These relationships can expand to include not only gifts but protection and a "no violence" policy towards this family that make arguments or litigation unthinkable. The focus is not on the value of the debt but on the value of the relationship.

While the concept of debt exists in the West it often involves more short-term reimbursement for favors done. "I'll pay you back." What Rudy had discovered on the bus was that Westerners do not seem to be comfortable when they feel they owe someone something, particularly if it is a long-term debt. If someone does something nice for you, you do everything possible to pay him back as quickly as possible. Once you have paid back your debt, depending on the magnitude of the favor accorded to you, you often have no lasting obligation.

As Rudy prepared to return to Senegal thinking this was is last trip to America, he did not know that years later, with the revival and recognition of the Baobab Orchestra, that he would be making many tours to cities across the US and Europe. The story of the Baobab Orchestra and its rebirth that allowed Rudy to travel repeatedly to the US and other world capitals, is one of those examples of reality being stranger than fiction.

"Who says that life can not have a 'happily ever after' ending for a group of middle aged musicians?" asked a feature writer from The Guardian, in a comprehensive article that told their story in October of 2002:

"...From the early seventies through the mid-eighties the Baobab Orchestra had been one of the dominant sounds of Dakar. It was the major dance music for Senegal's elite and their elegant wives, mistresses and girl-friends. It was a Cuban sound with a unique array of African elements from the Congo, Nigeria, and the rhythms of Senegal's Portuguese and Mandinka music as well as the neo-Islamic sounds of Senegalese Wolof *griots*, traditional praise singers. As Rudy said: "Africa respects its past in a way that Europe doesn't." In many ways, the music of the Baobab Orchestra was a Senegalese mosaic.' Every member of the group comes from a differ-ent place and a different tradition,' Rudy explained. 'We keep them all in balance and that has always been the essence of our music.' "

While the Baobab Orchestra remained Senegal's top group up to the late seventies, the balance of society was changing. The band barely noticed it, but out in the *quartiers populaires*, the sprawling, largely impoverished suburbs, where nobody cared about suits, ties or the cha-cha-cha, a pop revolution was underway, centered round a young singer named Youssou N'Dour, and a raw, new music called *mbalax*. The African percussion that had been subsumed into Baobab's gentle sound was brought right to the surface, alongside griot vocals, sax and rhythmic guitar; the linguistic medium was exclusively Wolof, the lingua franca of modern Senegal. This was followed by the emergence of Baaba Maal, who represented Senegal's second major linguistic group, the Haal Pulaar

"Ordinary people had been desperate for a form of music they felt was theirs," explained Rudy in his interview with The Observer. "Musicians like Youssou N'Dour and Baaba Maal provided that by making music which was much more obviously Senegalese. But this was only part of what the Baobab did."

Even at the top of their initial popularity, the Baobab Orchestra had always struggled to survive due to poor management and the irregularity of their contracts. These exceptional musicians were only poorly and erratically paid for their services despite their popularity. They had chronic problems making ends meet. After several unsuccessful attempts at improving their management, they eventually found themselves without gigs, and unwilling to adapt to the new trends. The Baobab Orchestra split in the mid eighties and so they remained for the next fifteen years. Despite several Paris-based albums, they had sadly never made it on the international scene. They had never received the international recognition they had deserved. They left a group of loyal, nostalgic fans who missed them, and continued to play their tapes and records.

They might have ended up a mere footnote in musical history were it not for the belief of a small number of Western enthusiasts who loved the music of the Baobab Orchestra and wanted to share the pleasure it had given them for so many years – and to make some money in the process. Senegal's Baobab Orchestra worked with World Circuit and a promoter named Nick Gold to achieve success similar to what he had accomplished with the highly successful revival of the Buena Vista Social Club in Cuba. Gold reconstituted an Afro-Cuban orchestra of neglected veterans playing the music they had played twenty years earlier. He turned them into an international music phenomenon. Gold harbored fantasies of getting the Baobab group back together as well. But it was only with the success of Buena Vista Social Club that he found the time and resources to try to do it.

Gold, in fact, succeeded in bringing together the original members of the Baobab Orchestra nearly 20 years after their break up. As he himself said: "Baobab are much more of a group than Buena Vista. Their musical chemistry is almost perfect...There is so much talent and creativity in Africa that it must win through in the end." And that, in fact, is what happened.

Rudy could not have imagined that at every stop where he performed in the US, in addition to enthusiastic fans of world music, he would always be greeted by former students from our center in Senegal, many of whom had driven miles to come to see him and to listen to him sing. Rudy had an extraordinary memory and never forgot a face. He understood the presence of these former students as a form of American "kolere", a demonstration of their loyalty, affection and gratitude for the gift of the language and cultural tools he had provided them with to allow them to fully appreciate their time in his wonderful country.

Rudy singing

The Baobab Orchestra

After one particularly successful concert at The Palace of Fine Arts in the Marina District of San Francisco in 2008, the guard at the stage door called Rudy out to tell him that a man named Scott Barker and his family were asking for him. "He says they are old friends."

Rudy stepped outside to find a smiling man with a twinkle in his eye. He recognized him as a student from a study abroad program in Senegal years earlier, though considerably older with slightly greying hair at the temples. He was accompanied by a beautiful black woman, obviously Senegalese, and two beautiful "café au lait" children.

"Scott," he said, "Babacar Ndiaye" and wrapped the student in a big bear hug.

"Rudy, you remember me and my Senegalese name?"

"Of course I do, we used to go out for beers and talk after classes! How could I forget?"

"I just drove up from LA with my family because I had to come to see you when I heard the Baobab was performing. I have spoken to my family about you so often!"

"This is my wife, Khady." Scott continued, indicating the lovely Senegalese woman by his side. Rudy greeted her warmly with kisses on both cheeks, asking her Senegalese family name as was the custom. She turned out to be from Rudy's region of the country and after a short conversation, they realized they were distant cousins.

"You really changed my life, Rudy!" said Scott.

"Me? What do you mean?"

"You may not remember, but I was having a very hard time adapting to Senegal when I first arrived and was considering going home. I had a massive case of culture shock."

"Yeah. I remember a couple of difficult days!" And they both laughed remembering Scott's initial meltdown.

"The Wolof you taught us and your insights into local customs helped me to get past my problems to the point where I could communicate and understand. But our one on one talks really helped me decide to stay for the entire eight months of my study abroad program. I came to appreciate Senegal and the Senegalese and became pretty fluent in French and Wolof. I came back on a consultation a couple of years later and tried to contact you but you were in the Casamance. It was then that I met Khady."

"And as you can see, we got married and had two children. None of this would have happened if it hadn't been for you!"

Rudy who loved kids bent over to greet the boys.

"What's your name?" he asked the smaller of the two boys who must have been 12.

"I'm Richard" he said perkily with a big smile, thrilled to be meeting the lead singer of the orchestra. He was a tan version of his father with the same sparkling eyes. "Can I have your autograph on my program?"

"Sure" said Rudy taking out his pen and writing "to my friend Richard".

Then Rudy turned to the older of the two boys who looked to be about 15 or 16 and had his mother's features. He was strikingly handsome.

"What's your name, young fellow?

"Rudy" he answered with a gentle smile.

9

GERARD CHENET

<><><><><><><><><><><><><><><><><><><><><><><><><><><><><><><><><><><><>

With today's bitter debates about immigration, it might be instructive to look back to the case of Haitian refugees and their contributions to Senegal.

B y the time I arrived in Senegal in the mid 1960's, Senegal had already become a haven, a place of asylum, for the Haitian intelligentsia fleeing the brutal Duvalier regime thanks to President Senghor's welcoming policies to his black diaspora, francophone brothers and sisters. For example, The poet, actor Lucien Lemoine and his much decorated wife, the actress Jacqueline Scott-Lemoine, and the poet and writer Jean Brierre (*Black Soul -1947 and La Source - 1956*) all rose to prominence in Senegal's cultural and artistic circles and were well known, appreciated and admired by the Senegalese population. Jean Brierre maintained an active career in public service and the cultural landscape of Dakar. He served in the Senegalese Ministry of Cultural Affairs, and played a major role in the 1966 World Festival of Negro Arts. Didi, the lovely, cultured wife of Jean Brierre, worked as a senior administrative assistant for generations of Peace Corps/

Senegal Directors, which gave us a privileged window on the Haitian community.

Among the Haitians intelligentsia who emerged in Senegal was the young and strikingly handsome Gerard Chenet.

Historian, teacher, actor, musician, sculptor, architect, ecologist, and visionary, Gérard Chenet is now over 80 years old and still living in Senegal. Despite his age, Chenet retains a youthful and extraordinary demeanor. He studied political science and African history, culminating with a doctoral thesis on the relationship between Germany and his native Haiti.

The young Gerard Chenet

Starting his career as a history teacher in Guinea, he later left Conakry to come to Senegal in the 1960s, where he worked as an advisor to the Ministry of Scientific Research in Dakar. He actively participated in an initiative of Senegal's first president, Leopold Sedar Senghor. the first World Festival of Black Arts (Féstival Mondial des Arts Nègres – April, 1966), along with his countrymen the Lemoines and Jean Brierre.

In the 1970's, Chenet acquired a small house in the Lébou fishing village of Toubab Dialao, located approximately 50 kilometers down the coast from Senegal's capital Dakar, where he gradually created his cultural complex named "Sobo Badé". There, he still indulges in his favorite activities: music, sculpture, and writing. In 2000, he got the idea of creating a retreat center where artists could simultaneously learn different subjects related to art (sculpture, theater, yoga, etc.). This second complex, situated three kilometers from Sobo Badé in the Dialao hills, was named Ndoungouma.

This chapter contains excerpts from an interview conducted with Gerard Chenet by Cheikh Thomas Faye and Mame Daour Wade and translated from French to English by Gary Engelberg and Katie Grimes for ACI's Yëgoo magazine in December 2011. Chenet shares memories from his youth, his vision of life, the secrets of this magical place called Sobo Badé, and its relationship with the villagers and his projects.

Chenet spent 4 years teaching African history in Guinea under Sékou Touré in the 1960's. When he was in Guinea, Chenet taught African history and started to write about the grand Imam El Hadj Oumar. He was very attracted to this person who reminded him of Haitian characters from the war: anti-slavery figures like Toussaint Louverture, Jean Jacques, the King Henri Rousseau.

El Hadj Omar made a great tour to the east, passing through Al Hazar University in Egypt, Algeria, and Fez in Morocco—all the religious centers of Islam. He also in some ways dominated the West African environment by his democratic and liberal doctrine, and by the patriotic sentiments that he professed to liberate Africa. From the beginning of colonization in West Africa to the time of Faidherbe, he brought together many people from Guinea to Mali, Boundou, the banks of the Faleme, through the "Petite Côte", where he settled for a while to recruit *talibés* (disciples) to conduct his jihad against the invasion of West Africa by the colonizers. He worked cautiously, starting first by Islamizing surrounding populations. While these populations already had their own cults and religions, the policy in West Africa at the time required a unifying factor. This unifying factor was Islam, and an Islam as conceived by El Hadj Omar.

Chenet sees the recent Arab spring as an example of youth revolting against the established order. He came out of a similar situation in Haiti. Democracy was gradually installed after a similar youth revolution in Haiti in 1946. Among this group of young students, there was René Dupestre,

Jacques Alexis, Girard Boncourt, and Chenet. Jacques Alexis was killed by the murderous Duvalier, and it was then that the group created a newspaper called La Ruche, in which they expressed their world vision. It was right after the Great War. Haiti knew neither political party nor union, nor freedom of the press; there was one government newspaper and no one was concerned with human rights. It was the gunmen who had the upper hand in Haiti, and Chenet's cohort succeeded in generating interest among the youth who rebelled against them.

Chenet was an actor in the first World Festival of Black Arts in 1966 at a time of cultural effervescence in Senegal where people discovered a modern form of the art practiced at that time that was not necessarily a divorce from traditional art forms but was very much inspired by President Senghor. Whenever Chenet intervened on the debates about Negritude, he would receive encouraging messages from President Senghor. That gave him the opportunity to see him, to visit him, and exchange correspondence, in particular, access to the writings of the time, poems on Toubab Dialao, and Elhaj Omar. Chenet found Senghor to be a very gracious and welcoming man. He welcomed all people and professionals who understood a bit of his thoughts, his doctrine on negritude. He also worked for the betterment of the poor. When he became the president of Senegal, he used all those who wanted to join him. It was the same thing in Guinea after independence when all the technical assistants left. Chenet was a part of that cohort of people who helped Sékou Touré rebuild the country.

Senghor helped promote the cultural effervescence in the country that he himself had promoted as a poet with the concept that "culture is at the beginning and at the end of development". Chenet always felt that we could not think of the development of Senegal without remembering him. It was upon Senghor's memory that the country is built, a memory of African art, African poetry, and traditional values that have experienced renewed expression.

Senghor spoke of cultural dialogue long before the globalization we are currently experiencing. He spoke about the universality of culture and the validity of this universality. He spoke of the mixing of cultures as an important factor in the reconstruction of well-being and development.

President Leopold Sedhar Senghor

Chenet felt that each group lives culture in its own manner. Each group lives in the shadow of its neighbors who also have a culture of their own. Culture is made up of memories from childhood. It is what we have lived, that with which we came into the world, our frustrations, our problems. Then, after birth, other illusions are added to what we have known since birth. The illusions distort our vision. These illusions for Chenet are malfunctions of the spirit.

Chenet settled in Toubab Dialao on the Petite Côte around 1970. There he created Sobo Badé an ideal, interesting place that allows one to reflect, write, isolate oneself, and to practice an artistic discipline. Today Sobo Badé is a very popular cultural complex. It was named after the Voodoo Gods of thunder and lightning, Sobo and Badé, the couple commanding light and sound. He chose the name as a sort of cultural guarantee, a memory he was trying to revive through the disciplines that he was already practicing at the time.

He and his family developed deep ties with the people of Toubab Dialao. Today they consider him like a Dad and call him *Papa Gerard*. The moment he moved there many things changed. First, he started practicing art and sculpture and many young people came to join him and to practice with him. His activities attracted many people, his friends first, and then a lot of people from the city who came to see the first building he constructed there. It was a small, modest house built out of recycled materials that he looked for everywhere: straw from African houses, marble, sumptuous wood floors, woodwork, bamboo, etc. He kept the momentum of an ecological vision going for anything he did in construction or building. Sobo Badé became an inescapable tourist attraction and a lot of people came to see the originality and the approach that Chenet had used for this establishment

Gerard Chenet today

In the year 2000, while exploring the hills around Toubab Dialao, he came across a space near a spring that provided fresh water all year round. He called it Ndoungouma. There was a large fig tree in the water and at the foot of this tree in the water, a big python. Chenet told himself that's how the myth of the creation of the world began. It's the serpent in paradise. He was inspired with a desire and a passion to recreate an environment here that he could share with visitors.

He spent every day working to build Ndoungouma while looking for funds to allow him to continue. He wanted to transform the place into a home for artists, a residence that would lodge artists and allow them to work on their artistic education according to their tastes and needs – an artist's workshop. He also created an ecological swimming pool and a playground for the children to make the place an ideal location.

Chenet was used to working with only limited means. He would rent out rooms to help finance his activities. He often supervised the work himself to reduce costs and with the help of his courageous wife, Sylvaine over the years, and a group of loyal workers, they have made impressive progress. They used laterite to construct Nubian vaults, an ancient technique practiced since the time of the Pharaohs that allows for a clean habitat, and is anti-seismic with good acoustics.

Lots of Senegalese and African architects and those from overseas are stunned and amazed by Sobo Badé. Even though Chenet undertook architecture without having the slightest notion about it, as a sculptor, he felt he was a sort of architect by profession. He describes architecture as a form of sculpture, a way of shaping space. Building a sculpture in stone or in marble involves the same principle, the same approach.

For Chenet, the first principle of art is above all else, rhythm. Rhythm is what the metabolism of our bodies is made of. Rhythm is in the human body, in the wind, and in space. It is especially to be found in social relations, in the trees, in the movement of the celestial bodies and the planets that orbit the sun, in our hearts. Our lives are rhythm. All of these rhythms produce an effect when they come together. For example: when you are facing a battery of drums, each rhythm is different. However, overall it creates music and produces harmonious sounds. That is the first principle of art, of life, and that is what Chenet practices. This is what allows him to go from one artistic activity to another. From writing, because the word is sacred, religious books produce the sacred word. It is also a call to rhythm as it is in the verses of the Bible and the Koran and in traditional and ancestral songs that express this concordance of rhythm.

Chenet feels we all depend on this. As living human beings, we depend on the different rhythms of the body, from the rhythms of the brain, to the rhythms of walking, through the organic rhythms. Should a single rhythm fail, it jeopardizes the entire organism, and in this case we find ourselves in the midst of a malfunction. Sickness reaches us because one of these rhythms has failed. That is what Chenet calls the universal concordance of rhythm. We need to have all of our rhythms in concordance. And that is why he says that the first principle of the rhythm of art and of life can be called the principle of universal concordance of rhythm.

For Chenet, human beings are largely responsible for current malfunctions in the environment. We have always said that the phenomena occurring in Bangladesh, Japan, Haiti, and elsewhere come from the fact that the atmosphere that envelopes the earth is affected by an acute malfunction caused by humans through the spread of toxic gases through the air until they reach the ozone layer. Chenet is convinced that the greater powers need to review their policies regarding this subject. The infinitely large is linked with the infinitely small. The tiny atom can affect the infinitely large. There is no animal that attacks the multitude of its kind: it is only human beings who make war while other animals do not.

10

DINING WITH BARACK

Presidents Barack Obama and Macky Sall

When I heard that President Obama was coming to Senegal where I have lived for close to fifty years, I pulled all the strings I could to be included somehow in the trip. Thanks to friends on both sides of the Atlantic, I was able to procure an invitation to the festivities surrounding President Obama's visit. This is the note I sent to them the next day:

H ad dinner with Barack and Michelle last night. Well, me and two hundred other chosen guests of Senegalese President Macky Sall and his wife in the elegant banquet hall of the Presidential Palace. Eighteen large, round tables of nine guests each with large golden Baobab plaques carrying the name of a Senegalese town faced a head table that ran the length of the room. I did not get to shake hands with my President, but I had a direct line of sight from my place to his, allowing me to follow his every move for most of the evening. It allowed me to create my own little fantasy that I was dining with Barack. I have been an avid supporter since he first emerged on the political scene in the US.

Although the boundless adoration for our young president and his lovely wife seems to have settled from the heady days of his first election into a more mature but no less real affection from the Senegalese people, the capacity of our presidential couple to connect with and charm their audience is very much intact. As an expatriate, I really wanted to thank them for restoring our image in the world.

Michelle and Barack Obama

The speeches of mutual respect and affection were moving. In "Dreams of my Father" Barack had written about once meeting a Senegalese migrant worker in a bus in Spain whose ambition was to bring his wife to join him. They shared coffee and warm exchanges. Well, in an elegant gesture of true *teranga* (hospitality), the Senegalese government had gone to the trouble of locating this individual and bringing him to the dinner in a poignant reunion with the man who had since become President of the United States.

Baba Maal and his three singers praised Obama in a very moving traditional griot (praise singer) style that clearly touched the American president, even though his access to the meaning of the words being sung was somewhat limited. But if you ever doubted that souls can speak to each other, you would have been convinced last night if you had looked into Obama's eyes as Baaba Maal was singing.

Praise Singer Baaba Maal

As the elegant six-course meal progressed, then Minister of Culture, Youssou Ndour, donned his role of international star to sing about the future of Africa, praise the American president and return once again to sing his classic "Birima" to the delight of the audience. At one point I could feel some excitement in one corner of the room and turned to see the two First Ladies gradually making their way behind the long head table towards Youssou and his drummers, with rhythmic steps and elegant movements. But when Barack rose to join them he not only brought the audience to their feet but drew the more reserved Senegalese president into the dance. Probably the first time the Senegalese public has seen their president dance!

Thank you all for pulling strings to get me invited. I did not go to work this morning. I slept late and had a late breakfast, and was sad to watch the news as Obama's plane left for South Africa where he will hopefully see the ailing Nelson Mandela. But my morning has been filled with my memories of dining with Barack.

11

ANNIE GOES TO AFRICA

◇◇

M y Uncle Charlie, her brother, used to call her Anna. Dad called her Annie, when he wasn't using one of the many endearing terms that had become automatic after 60 years of marriage. On her birth certificate, her name was misspelled as Aimee. Her real name was Anne. She was my mother.

Anne passed away at sunset on Thursday February 20, 1997 at the age of 90. In 1992 after losing her husband (my Dad), and the second of her three sons (my older brother) in the same year, she was devastated. Most of all, she felt alone and depressed as many of the aged in America do in a society that does not often value them or their contributions.

She had been one of those "new women" who came out of the "home" after World War II and joined the work force in the 50's. I remember when she decided to go back to work and the young child that I was no longer had his mother at his beck and call all day long. For over thirty years she worked her way up in banking, ending her career as an assistant vice president before retiring to Florida as so many New Yorkers do when they get older.

Except for an occasional trip to Miami or New Orleans in the course of her career, Anne had never been a traveler. In 86 years she had never left the United States. So I was surprised when she finally accepted my invitation to come to visit me in Senegal where I had been living since 1965. Given her advanced age and fragile health, I invited Donna, a nurse, to accompany her on the ten-day trip to Dakar. We had met Donna at the hospital during the course of Mom's repeated illnesses, as she grew older. Donna had been particularly caring to her and had become a family friend, almost like the daughter Mom never had. Every time Mom had to return to the hospital, Donna was there to care for her.

When Anne and Donna finally arrived in Dakar in November of 1992, Mom told me about the Catch 22 preparations she had gone through trying to get here. I asked her to write it all down. I still remember the day she read it to me during one of my visits before she died. She laughed heartily at her memories of what must have been a very frustrating period. A few months ago when I was cleaning up my home office over Christmas vacation, I came across two and a half pages of yellow foolscap covered with my mother's hasty scribble describing her ordeal. I brought it back to Senegal with me along with pictures of her trip as a souvenir of one of the best things I had ever done for her – and for me. I loved her account of the preparations for what she called the BIG trip:

Dec 7, 1992

My son has been living in Senegal for 27 years and decided it was time for his 86-year old mother to visit him. But the experiences I encountered trying to get the necessary shots, passport, and other documents made me wonder at times if I was ever going to make it.

The problems started with the birth certificate which I sent for to New York in late May or early June. Sometime in August I was notified that they had no birth certificate for Anne Perla (my maiden name). I must admit this did not surprise me since I had had the same experience 64 years earlier when I applied for my marriage license! Now started an endless round of phone calls, winding up in the archives and finally getting a stamped certified birth certificate in mid-September. Between my father's Yiddish accent when he went to register my birth, and the ears of the registrar who was probably Italian, I had been transformed from Anne Perla into Aimee Periller on my birth certificate!

Now came time for the passport. After 10 or 12 phone calls I was told that the Pompano Beach post office was the place. I called and received a passport application, which I filled out immediately. I then made an appointment for my yellow fever shot at the Board of Health for Friday. On Thursday, one day before the appointment, I received a letter from the Department of State telling me that I could not have a passport because of a discrepancy of information between my application and my birth certificate. I called and was told it would take two months for a legal name change from Aimee Periller to Anne Perla or vice versa.

By now a hysterical old lady began to wonder whether the Fates were saying not to go, or what? I called my nephew and his wife who took a day off from work, and picked me up at 8 a.m. the next day. Off we went to the Board of Health for my yellow fever shot only to learn that they were out of vaccine! They directed us to Sunrise Medical, many miles away where I got my shot, but for $49 instead of the $25 I was supposed to pay at the Board of Health.

Then we headed off for Miami and the State Department, another hour's drive away. We got there with as many papers as we could muster: proof of Anne Perla having gone to public school, a marriage license, social security card and driver's license which unfortunately had the wrong date of birth on it. (I had never changed it because even though I had had a driver's license for years I had never driven!) Well, after a long interrogation, I left the State Department feeling sad and discouraged.

But three days later, by some miracle, I received a passport and shouted to the world that I had made it! I immediately called Dakar to let my son know....

Annie on the flight to Dakar

Anne or Anna (or Aimee if you prefer) and nurse Donna had a great trip. They took a flight to New York and spent the night and most of the next day in an airport hotel to let Mom recuperate from the first leg of her journey. Then, late that afternoon they boarded the flight for Dakar.

When their plane landed, I was waiting for them on the tarmac. It was before 9/11 and airport security in Senegal was a lot less stringent in those years. I waited for what seemed like an eternity as all the passengers deplaned descending the huge staircase that had been wheeled out from the terminal. The flow of passengers ended and I began to worry that something had happened. Finally, my mother's bent silhouette appeared at the door of the plane and accompanied by Donna she exited into the morning sun and began her labored descent, one step at a time. Looking down at her feet and holding on to the rail on one side and to Donna's arm on the other, she gradually made it down to the tarmac. As soon as her feet hit the ground, she stood up straight, punched the air like a New York Knicks player who had just scored a basket and said "Yeah!" Obviously, a major accomplishment.

Then she turned to the Pan Am agent waiting at the foot of the stairs and said "Hello Gary." She did not have dementia but I could tell she was tired from the trip and a bit confused. Once we got that misunderstanding cleared up, and she remembered what I looked like, we proceeded to the terminus in a car provided by the airline.

By some good fortune, my colleague's mother (about ten to fifteen years younger than my mother) and her friend were also visiting, so with Donna and my Mom they formed a foursome, a kind of support group that moved around together much of the time and occasionally sat to talk and to process what was going on or just shoot the breeze in familiar English – a respite from the constant flow of French and Wolof that was going on around them. We had great Senegalese rice meals together, often around a common bowl that our mothers loved but nurse Donna could not handle for hygienic reasons. We gave her her own separate plate. In the evenings we prepared Western food and ate together from plates around the table.

One day I took Mom around Dakar sightseeing. We got to the ocean road called the little corniche or *Corniche Ouest*, where lots of houses and hotels are built into the side of the cliff. At one point she said she was thirsty so I stopped at the lovely Savana Hotel thinking I would show her another corner of Dakar with a great ocean view. We could sit around their Olympic Pool and have a coke. I had forgotten about the huge number of stairs that we needed to descend and worse, that we needed to climb back up when we finished. She mumbled something about a lot of stairs but did not complain while we were there. That evening with our little group of co-tourists and friends sitting around my round table finishing our dinner, she wryly announced that "My son tried to kill me today!"

Donna was a tall, strong athletic woman who loved to play softball. She belonged to an amateur team in Florida and played regularly. Over the weekend, when she mentioned that she would really like to get some exercise, we got permission from the American Embassy for her join their softball team for their Sunday game. She turned out to be the star first baseman when an opposing player hit a ball picked up by the shortstop who threw it to her wide and she made an incredible stretch catch with her foot on the base that brought everyone, including my mother, to their feet, applauding.

We travelled down to Mbour and the most accessible tourist area on the Petite Côte where we spent the night in a hotel near the ocean. We had croissants and *thé au lait* for breakfast and walked slowly along the beach together reminiscing about things long forgotten while Donna stayed behind to nap after a difficult night of caring for my mother. We laughed about the time my Dad, when he was alive, had been interviewed by a newspaper reporter about living in a retirement village. He told her it was like living in Death Valley! When she quoted him in the headline of the article she wrote, all the neighbors came to complain to my father that he was ruining the property values!

Mom saw the Senegalese fishermen and their colorful pirogues and watched, after a nap later that day, as they pulled in their nets filled with fish. We passed some of the big tourist hotels that had gone up along the shore that reminded her of Miami. The water was too cold for swimming, but, for a long time, we just sat silently and watched the ebb and flow of the ocean together knowing, but not saying, that she was not going to be around much longer. Quality time. We drove through the main street of the town of Mbour that she later referred to as "the slums," and then took a leisurely ride back to Dakar.

For ten days Anne and Donna were the happy recipients of concentrated Senegalese 'teranga' (hospitality)– seemingly unending visits of friends who were curious to meet the woman who had given birth to me, invitations to meals, warm embraces, sometimes laughing, sometimes tearful, and gifts of bracelets, necklaces, clothing, small wooden statues, copper wall pictures…lots of broken English and sign language. In a gesture of affection reserved for older mothers, some of the Senegalese women visiting instinctively sat right next to her on the couch with their thighs touching so that she could feel their presence, something Mom seemed to warm to after the initial shock of having her space violated.

Friends came to the house with their wives, babies and young children. I was particularly pleased that she got a glimpse of my relationships with my Senegalese friends that had been built up over the years. She was told how they felt about me. For them it was a chance to tell my mother – and me – how much I meant to them. It is very embarrassing, but whenever you do anything good for anybody in Senegal, they insist on talking about it, over and over, whenever the occasion presents itself. They keep reminding you and letting you know, and everybody around them who happens to be present, that they haven't forgotten and are grateful. It took me years to stop feeling embarrassed when they did this. I would turn red as a tomato. Reputation is important in Senegal and by contributing to your good reputation by telling others about your good works, they are, in a sense, returning your gift. "Good deeds people do for you should be talked about..." *kuu lay def lu baax, dan koy wax* — they would tell me in Wolof when I tried to quiet them down. The tone in their voice translated as an unspoken admonishment "Don't be ridiculous, any child would know that! Why shouldn't we talk?"

In fact, in this culture, the act of visiting someone is in itself a gift. People honor you and your home by coming to visit you. It is not the host who is doing something kind by receiving a guest. It is the guest who is doing something kind by coming to visit. Although she did not fully understand the intricacies of the social mechanisms, my Mom knew she was being honored every day that she was here.

The Senegalese immediately adopt another posture when they are dealing with older people – especially when they see white hair. They become respectful and solicitous. They lower their eyes and try to anticipate your every need. They remind you how much you have to offer them by sharing your long experience with them and they listen intently when you talk. Especially when you tell them about your life experiences that occurred at times before they were born. Maintaining the connection between the present and the past is a cultural priority for the Senegalese. But that is the subject of another book. A wolof proverb reminds people that it is good to have older people in the community – *Mag matne baay cim réew* - and that the word of an old person will be quickly confirmed in reality - Waxu mag du fanaan alla – the word of an old person does not spend the night in the bush.

Actually, the Senegalese are very conscious of age, in general. Among siblings, it is important to always remember who is older. The younger sibling owes respect to the older sibling. They are regarded as junior parents and given the same respect you would give a mother or father, especially when the brother or sister is the oldest in the family. An older sibling can send a younger sibling on an errand or give instructions just as a parent would. They will often carry their younger siblings on their backs when they are infants or small children just the way their parents would or take them to their first day in school. This hierarchy is maintained through life and they do not hesitate to discipline their younger brothers or sisters when necessary. The younger sibling can never catch up to the older sibling, but can exercise his older brother or sister status on his/her younger brother or sister. When two people argue, it is not unusual for one to say to the other "*Hé maa la mag!*" (Hey, I am older than you – meaning you should respect me). In an interesting cultural twist, in the case of twins, Senegalese believe that the first born is the younger of the two twins because his or her older brother or sister still in the womb sent him/her to check things out, a privilege only older siblings enjoy.

There is a whole system here where it seems as though all of the younger people in society have been given the responsibility of monitoring your aging process. You do not feel it as a younger person yourself, but as soon as you begin to gain a certain maturity, younger people spontaneously begin to call you *tonton* (uncle in French and Wolof). You may not realize you have changed, but they do. The first time you are called *tonton* is always a shock. You look around at first to see whom they are talking to before you realize that you are now the *tonton*. And by some strange coordinated choreography, all young people begin calling you *tonton* at the same time. But that is nothing compared to the surprise several years later on when someone calls you "père" (father) or papa for the first time! It happened to me unexpectedly one day when I was sitting in the front seat of a car on the passenger's side with my window down. We stopped at a traffic light where beggars gather and often ask passengers in their captive audience for alms. One of them came up to me and assuming that because I was white, I only spoke French he said: "Père, charité." Who is he calling "père?" I thought.

Finally, when you begin to walk more slowly, with labored steps, and your hair begins to turn white, the younger people all simultaneously begin to call you *maam*, which in Wolof means grandfather or grandmother. Your married friends start bringing their little children to visit *maam* regularly but make sure that they do not tire you out. So it was perfectly understandable that when my Mom was here, everyone came to my house with their kids to pay a visit *Maam Anna*. For the kids it was a great, mysterious adventure. "Yes, *Papa Gary* has a mother!" Wide-eyed and curious about this *toubab* grandmother, and dutifully following their parents' instructions, the kids gave her baby kisses on her wrinkled cheek. In return, they were rewarded with kisses and warm hugs and baby talk in English that they somehow seemed to understand, nodding their heads to every question she asked. They were mesmerized by this old, white lady with kind eyes and fluffy, white hair wearing a floral housecoat, who regaled them with little gifts for kids that she had brought from the US and kept pulling out of her seemingly bottomless pockets.

The parting wish proffered to old people is always "Yal na nga yagg suñu kanaam" "May God keep you present before us for a longtime to come" and you respond "Amine" but you are left with the subtle reminder that because you are old, you can die any time now. In a country where so many people young and old die of health issues long resolved in the West, there is a heightened awareness of how precarious life is and how close death can be. Thus the need to ward it off with frequent wishes for long life.

I know today that I will never be able to share my life here with her again or to share her with my friends.

Anne loved every minute of the attention she received. She was delighted. Coming from her lonely existence in Florida in an old people's retirement community, still grieving for her husband of sixty years and her second son who died too soon, she was pleased to be surrounded by younger people and their children. It had the same feel as ten days of Thanksgiving or Passover when the family came to visit - only this time she was doing the visiting and her "family" was suddenly Senegalese. And people were cooking for her, and catering to her every need, for a change.

A very dear, Senegalese friend once told me a story about her grandmother. In a country where the women of the house often sit together to prepare the day's cooking by cleaning the uncooked rice in large trays, pulling out the tiny pebbles and impurities and gossiping about the days news, older women have problems participating when their eyesight fails and they can no longer distinguish between the rice kernels and the pebbles. Seeing her grandmother's growing frustration, my friend prepared a special tray of rice kernels into which she mixed a package of large black beans so that her grandmother could continue feeling useful, sitting with the other women, gossiping about the day's events and picking out the "stones".

It occurred to me in re-reading Mom's notes years later that the preparations for the trip may have been as important as the trip itself. They pulled her out of her lethargy and depression. She was no longer the victim. She was no longer alone. She once again became the persistent bank executive forcing a hostile bureaucratic world to respond to her requests. Like my friend's grandmother, she had been re-empowered.

But Anne saw it a bit differently. A couple of years before she died, when we were reminiscing about her voyage to Senegal, I asked her what she remembered from her trip. She responded without hesitation: "They sure know how to treat old people over there!"

12

THE REFUGEE

◇◇◇

*In 2001, ACI worked with the Fund for African Relief and Education (FARE) to help support the wave of young Sierra Leonean refugees pouring into Dakar to escape the violence in their country. Many of them left their country in small boats to escape Freetown when it was under attack by the rebels. Many landed in neighboring Guinea and some made their way up to Dakar where they slept in the market place or car parks until they got settled. "**The Refugee**," first published in ACI's Yegóo magazine of March 2001, is a poem inspired by that experience.*

> Asleep beneath the market stall,
>
> A flattened carton for his bed,
>
> Rays of street light through the table slats
>
> Stripe his man-child face with strange designs.
>
> Dreams of fear invade his troubled sleep:
>
> The panic of the prey pursued.
>
> Thumps and gunshots, screams and flames,

The crunch of rifle butt against young ribs.

Cold and crushed in a cramped, damp boat
Battered by an angry black sea.
The smell of wet wood assails his nose.
The gift of sleep can no more numb his pain.

Gnawing hunger fills his thoughts.
His mother's face haunts his heavy heart.
He turns to see the flames and smoke
Now silent, fading in the distance and the night.

He starts and jumps quickly onto the beach
From his place on a plank in the boat
To feel the wet sand of another place
Beneath his feet, between his toes.

He walks alone in a crowd of strangers
Seeking
But not finding
Kind eyes to share his grief.

Fleeing Sierra Leone

13
LAST DAYS

◇◇

S oon after a foreigner arrives in Senegal, one Senegalese or another will
invariably ask: "What is your Senegalese name?" And if you don't have
an answer they will say: "Well, now you are Ibrahima Diop" or "You are
Aissatou Diallo" and that usually becomes your official Senegalese name
for the rest of your stay in Senegal.

By giving the foreigner a Senegalese name not only do the Senegalese
let you know you are welcome, but it allows them to relate to you because
names carry information on ethnicity, caste, family connections, regional
origins, and much more. This allows Senegalese to situate the foreigner in
the local system and activate all the established conventions, relationships
and behaviors prescribed in Senegal's intricate social architecture.

The family name is repeated in greetings usually followed by an hon-
orific suffix particular to each name. It would be the equivalent of meeting John Smith in English and saying: "Smith, Smith, Smith The Tiger."
A Senegalese greeting me, as Ibrahima Ndiaye, will say: *"Ndiaye, Ndiaye,
Ndiaye Diatta Ndiaye"* or *"Gayndé Ndiaye"* (Ndiaye the lion) and I will
respond *"Diop, Diop, Diop Juba, Diop"* (Diop with a tuft like the black

crowned crane). Everyone in Senegal knows these suffixes by heart, although the young people in the cities are starting to forget them: *"Touré Mandé Moré"* (refers back to the Mandé empire), *"Sarr Gelem"* (Sarr the Camel), or my favorite *"Seck, Seen Ginaar"* (Seck, your chickens), which is short for *"Seck Seen ginaar amul buñ ci kaaw amul buñ ci suuf"* (Seck, your chickens do not have upper or lower teeth). Some of them refer back to family totems, others to historical facts about the origins of the family and still others I have yet to fully understand. It makes for great subjects of conversation with older people who know the origins of these suffixes.

Other conventions require that somebody named Ndiaye meeting somebody named Diop, for example, will immediately start teasing saying: "Diop, you are my slave" or "You really like to eat rice, don't you?" or any number of other friendly insults. The person named Diop will immediately retort, creating much laughter, backslapping and relaxing the discomfort of meeting someone you do not know for the first time. These exchanges exist for different pairs of names called *"kaal"* and everyone knows them (Gueye/Niang, Seck/Gaye, Ndiaye/Diop…). This "teasing cousins" relationship warms the atmosphere by indicating we are all connected, and facilitates initial contact even between strangers or consolidates existing relationships.

Anthropologist Dennis Galvan tells us:

"Beyond these regularized insults, the rhetoric of joking kinship also prohibits open conflict between these metaphorical cousins. Joking kin are usually expected, in spite of (or perhaps because of…) the teasing, to show special willingness to support or provide material resources when their 'cousins' are in need. Moreover, it is widely expected that joking kin are especially suited to intervene in the internal conflicts of the group with whom they are paired as cousins."

Although I cannot remember who gave me my Senegalese name, I know that I was baptized "Ibrahima Ndiaye" and that Senegalese name has stuck with me for over fifty years, to this day. I have played the "kaal" card hundreds of times telling anyone I meet named Diop that they eat too much rice, and it really works, especially coming from a *toubab* (white person).

Peace Corps volunteers today are mostly placed in rural areas and with Senegalese families so they often take on the name of their families. In my case, having been assigned to the capital city to teach in the Teacher's College, I had lots of friends but lived in an apartment and did not immediately have that Senegalese family connection that rural volunteers immediately acquire. But some anonymous acquaintance among my initial contacts took care of that for me deciding I would be "Ibrahima Ndiaye," and I had my Senegalese name.

As a Volunteer in Dakar, I spent some time with a young men's social group called "The Jamaicans". Many of the members were from Dakar's Medina and quite a few were concentrated on Rue 13. And it was on Rue 13 that I met my lifelong friend Pape Seck and through him, a magical, young, primary school teacher named El Hadji Sarr who was to become my Senegalese brother. He was small of stature but muscular and athletic which gave the impression that he was much bigger than his actual size. He and Pape Seck were friends and teammates on the Gorée soccer team and El Hadj was staying with Pape Seck's family on Rue 13. We immediately hit it off and, in the course of conversation he invited me to visit his family on the island of Gorée off the coast of Dakar where they lived.

The next weekend, I took the ferry to Gorée called the *chaloupe* with our lovely volunteer Secretary, Darcy Neill. She had recently been transferred to Dakar when her Peace Corps program in Gabon was closed and she was still discovering Senegal. With a great sense of humor and a contagious laugh, she was a pleasure to know and invariably brightened and lightened conversations she participated in. As the oldest of many children, she had a "take charge" mentality and was a great mediator. She was striking because she had long dark hair with a two-inch wide blond stripe at a time when fashion did not yet allow that kind of color mixing.

El Hadji met us on the dock and took us through the winding, sandy streets of Gorée to the family compound where his father and his two mothers lived with their children, nieces and nephews and other members of the extended family. The short walk took quite a while as he stopped to greet and talk to everyone he met on the way and to introduce his new American friends. That day was the beginning of my relationship with what was to become my Senegalese family, the Sarr family and with the people of Gorée Island.

We were welcomed with great interest and extraordinary warmth by all the members of the family, young and old, and with particular curiosity by the little ones who had not yet had a lot of close contact with many white people. Darcy was a great asset and had people already cultur- ally disposed to teasing and

Yaay Sambou

laughter, enjoying each other immensely. We were called to share their meal and drank *attaya* lying on mattresses and mats around the sandy compound.

El Hadji's mother, Yaay Sambou, a diminutive woman from the Casamance and first wife of El Hadji's father, Pa Souleymane "Bouna" Sarr, became my Senegalese mother over the years. She had three children with Pa Bouna: a daughter named Diaw Sarr, El Hadji and a younger brother named Ousmane. A picture of Yaay Sambou hangs in my house to this day even though she died many years ago. Her oldest daughter, and my big sister Diaw Sarr, has gradually replaced her as the matriarch of the family.

Darcy and I began to make regular trips to Gorée on weekends and holidays and sometimes spent the night in the Sarr compound, drinking tea and talking under the stars with three or four of us sharing a mattress when we finally fell asleep. We would visit the homes of friends of the Sarrs, watch basketball and soccer matches played in the sand, and attend young people's dances with a combination of Reggae, Afro-Cuban salsa, and the latest Western and Senegalese music blasting out of huge speakers. We would swim off the main beach, climb the Castel and even go out occasionally in a fishing pirogue. We came to look forward to the weekends and holidays when we could get away to this little island paradise with our new-found Senegalese friends.

With time, we learned to differentiate the members of the family and understand, in most cases, who was related to whom and how. Initially, it was difficult because a new person would be presented as "my brother" or "my sister", but we later learned that they did not share the same parents. In our terms they were first or second cousins. But they considered themselves brothers and sisters. In fact, the person they called "father" or "mother" would often turn out to be their uncle or aunt (in our terms).

If I tried to describe each member of the family and their connections as well as all the other interesting Goreens we met in the course of this relationship with the Sarr family, it would take volumes and I am not sure that my memory or my writing skill would allow me to do them all justice. Each one was a character and worth writing about.

I have always admired my friends and colleagues who have great memories. They somehow avoid the reduction of past experiences over time. For me, time flows over my experiences like water over stones smoothing out the rough edges and leaving me with polished nuggets of shiny but imprecise memories. I can often remember the essentials but find it difficult sometimes to remember the details.

At one point, I thought about changing my Senegalese name to "Sarr" in order to indicate that I was really part of my new family, but I had had the name of Ibrahima Ndiaye for a couple of years before meeting them, and had been introduced to the family as "Ibrahima Ndiaye", so I decided to keep my name. As I got to know the family members better, I learned that many had other surnames. Yaay Sambou's children from previous marriages were named Ndiaye and Diagne and Yaay Mai's children from a previous marriage were named Ba and Mbengue but they were all considered to be brothers and sisters within the Sarr family.

But of the literally hundreds of family members and Goreen friends Darcy and I got to know through our relationship with the Sarr family, certain have played critical roles and continue to play important roles in my life 45 years later.

After El Hadji left to play soccer in France, I continued to visit the family on a regular basis. I gradually took on some of El Hadji's responsibilities

The young Saaku Sarr

as an older brother of the family, functions that El Hadji would have performed had he been here. One of those functions was looking out for the welfare of the younger siblings and helping them surmount the obstacles of life they invariably encountered.

Mame Mamour "Saaku" Sarr was the 15 year-old son of Yaay Maimouna Sene, Papa Bouna's second wife with whom he had two surviving sons "Saaku" and Moustapha and one daughter, Ndeye Coumba. Their mother was known lovingly as Yaay Mai. She and Yaay Sambou lived in peace as co-wives and were, in fact, complicit in many things. In our terms, Saaku was El Hadji's half brother. In their terms he was his brother.

The unusual name "Saaku" which basically translates as "old sack" was part of a Senegalese tradition that gave the children of mothers who had previously miscarried an ugly name so that the spirits would think they had no value and would not take them away. This is why you meet people named *"Ken Begul"* (nobody wants her), *"Begouma"* (I don't want her), *"Sagaar"* (old rag) or *"Saraax"* (something given away for charity). As an infant, Saaku was allegedly placed in a sack on one of the old stone walls of Gorée as his mother uttered the prayer for the survival of her baby: "May he stay as long as the stones of Gorée."

When I first met the family, Saaku was a student in Dakar's prestigious Lycée Van Vollenhoven, subsequently renamed Lycée Lamine Gueye when the names of colonial heroes were replaced with those of national ones. Saaku was bright, athletic and loved to speak English. He seemed to be doing quite well at school and had a personality that made him very popular. One day, I found Saaku sitting around when he should have been in school. He explained that he, and his entire class, had been expelled by one of their teachers for some alleged lack of respect. The punishment seemed heavy to me no matter what the offense. In effect, the teacher was ruining the academic career and probably the future of an entire class of young people.

At the time I was in charge of TEFL (Teaching English as a Foreign Language) programs for Peace Corps in Senegal and knew all the directors of the private Catholic schools where most of our teachers were assigned. I could not stand by and let a promising kid like Saaku be relegated to a menial job or sent out into the rural areas to farm peanuts. I went to see Papa Bouna and offered to pay Saaku's school fees at the Catholic College Sacré Coeur that also had a majority of Moslems in the student body. The College had an excellent reputation. He agreed and a few days later, Saaku was admitted.

The next weekend, Papa Bouna called me and explained that it was very difficult and expensive for Saaku to commute from the Island of Gorée every school day that required a ferry ride before taking public transport to the other end of the city. Since Sacré Coeur was within walking distance of my house, Pa Bouna asked if Saaku could come to live with me and come back to Gorée on the weekends.

I had not foreseen that possibility. I realized it was a measure of the trust that the family had in me. I agreed, a bit reluctantly, and overnight, I went from being a 23-year-old bachelor living alone to the "father" of a fifteen year old boy! I had a three-bedroom villa and there was certainly enough room, and I had the means to house and feed him. But until then, I had lived a self-centered life and had not yet been called upon to take on a parental role and give generously of myself to raise another human being. So in that sense, it was a great adventure and an opportunity for personal growth. Culturally, his presence at my house created new contacts with people I otherwise would never have met, particularly his young friends at school and in the neighborhood. He also helped me to understand all sorts of things about Senegalese culture.

From me he learned about tuna salad, egg salad, omelettes, hamburgers and spaghetti. Luckily we had Senegalese food at noon so he was not too disoriented. I'm not sure which of my American ways he had the most difficulty getting used to. We did speak lots of English, and I think my curiosity and constant questions about the structure of Wolof rubbed off on him and gave him an even greater interest in language and linguistics and language teaching. He later taught Wolof and French to our American students and today teaches Spanish and French in an American High School in California.

Saaku did very well in the well-disciplined system of a Catholic School and a supportive home environment, and he was soon at the top of his class. Several memories of his time there stand out. One afternoon, the school that was impeccably run by Canadian "brothers," organized a visit by a professional mime to come and do a show for the students. That evening, Saaku returned home enchanted and entertained us by basically duplicating the entire performance. It was then that I realized what incredible talent he had as an actor and comedian.

On another day, the American basketball player Kareem Abdul-Jabbar came to Senegal through the US Information service. As part of his visit, the Embassy wanted to organize a trip to Gorée to see the slave house and meet with young people from the island. They called to ask if I could suggest a young English-speaking guide. I immediately proposed Saaku since he was from Gorée and spoke English. I made the mistake of pulling him out of school for a day without consulting the Canadian brothers. The Canadian brother prefect turned Saaku away for truancy the next day and asked for a written explanation for his absence if I wanted him to be accepted back into school. I wrote an apologetic note explaining that I thought the educational value of serving as a guide and translator for a celebrated American basketball player was worth a day of missed classes. The Prefect did not appreciate my decision, but did, nevertheless, allow Saaku to return to class.

Saaku was eventually invited back to the Lycée as one of the top students in the private Catholic school system in Dakar. He went on to marry a beautiful Senegalese woman of Moroccan descent and have two children. They later divorced, and today he lives in California with his American wife and his Senegalese children but spends at least a month in Senegal every year.

At one point, 12-year old Paul Coly came to join us. He was the son of a relative of Yaay Sambou who had also been living in the Gorée compound as one of the family children. His primary school experience had failed miserably, and he did not have much to do other than run errands. He came to visit Saaku, partly out of affinity and partly out of curiosity, and gradually became a regular visitor until he, too, eventually moved in.

Over the years I managed to give him some basic skills like reading and writing, simple accounting, putting lists into alphabetical order, and learning to drive. I would send him to do the shopping and ask him to report back on what he had spent and how much each item had cost. He learned to do errands and go to the bank to cash checks. He got to know all the back streets in Dakar and how to avoid traffic during rush hour. He was conscientious, efficient and always available to help. This all made him employable despite his limited education and able to earn his livelihood. He is now, 45 years later, approaching retirement from his job as an appreciated driver and messenger at our NGO.

Over the months, various other family members came to join us. Each one brought something special. I loved the company and the fun and all the things I was learning about Wolof and Senegalese humor and customs. I had lost my independence and privacy but had gained so many other things. I had a great Senegalese cook and would host big, Senegalese lunches around a bowl on mats in the back yard where my American colleagues, friends and visitors would meet the members of my Senegalese family. At one point, there were seven family members living with me. After a while it became difficult both in terms of responsibility and expenses.

I went to see Yaay Sambou, most embarrassed to tell her that the arrangements had become difficult for me and I did not know what to do. Without reproach or judgment of any kind she said kindly in Wolof with great simplicity and wisdom: *"Danga yikkiti linga atanul. War nga tekk dara."* (You are carrying more on your head than you can bear. You have to put something down.) That allowed me to negotiate changes that made the situation easier without compromising my relations with the family that I had come to treasure.

El Hadji's brother Souleymane was called Bouna. He was named after El Hadji's father and was, in our terms, El Hadji's second cousin. He was described to me as the son of Pa Bouna's brother, Abdoulaye Sarr, who was in fact the son of the brother of Pa Bouna's father (Pa Bouna's cousin, in our terms). Bouna also lived in the Gorée compound as a brother in the extended family. He had received a military scholarship to study medicine. Since he had classes at the University Hospital, also a stone's throw from my home, he too stayed at my house for a while to prepare his exams.

Bouna was quiet, polite, reserved and very hard working. He became a military doctor assigned at one point to the fire department. He went on to study Emergency Medicine in Antwerp for several years. He was chosen as one of the military doctors who accompanied then President Abdou Diouf on official missions. He also became the trusted physician of Senegal's First Lady, Elizabeth Diouf. Bouna grew over the years into a perceptive diagnostician and a highly intuitive doctor, very much like a traditional healer. He had a flair for "feeling" his patients' illness. "Doctor Bouna" (Colonel Doctor Souleymane Sarr) has remained my close friend, my brother and my personal physician until this day.

And through Bouna we got to know his childhood friend on Gorée, Souleymane Keita who became the leading figure in contemporary abstract art in Senegal. When we met him in 1967 in his early 20's, he had already been studying under the master Senegalese painter Iba Ndiaye (1928-2008) since the age of 13. He had set up a studio in the side of the "Castel" that makes up half of Gorée Island. It was once Fort Saint Michel built on a castle begun in 1530 on the top of the rocky coast and served later as World War II fortifications complete with huge canons that covered the entrance to Dakar harbor. Today all the nooks and crannies of the fortifications have been squatted by young artists and Rastafarians who produce batiks and paintings and have created vegetable gardens across the plateau of the fortress alongside its old cannons and bunkers. At the time, the Castel was largely uninhabited except for an occasional *"fou"* (crazy person).

Souleymane Keita was one of the few people at the time who had made the Castel his workplace. His studio was filled with Senegalese artifacts that inspired him: paintings, canvas frames and the smell of oil paints, acrylics and linseed oil. I was moved by the creativity and talent of this very young painter and by his commitment to his art.

On several subsequent trips back to the States I would buy acrylic paints and brushes at a favorite little old art store on Coney Island Avenue just off Avenue J in Brooklyn where I had grown up and bring them back for Souleymane. It was across the street from the barber shop where I used to get my hair cut as a schoolboy and down the block from the Jewish Yeshiva of Flatbush where I did my first eight years of school. Darcy and I talked about Souleye Keita's work to many people in the American community and helped contribute to his growing popularity, though word of his work had already begun to spread.

In 1969, Souleye organized his first solo exhibition. Two years later, he showed his work in Nouakchott, Mauritania and proceeded from there to travel the world. He and his work were welcomed for exhibitions at galleries across Africa, the United States, Japan, Mexico, France, and Canada over the next twenty years (1972–1991).

Souleye's work was grounded in abstraction. He used symbols to express his connections to spirituality, his personal experience, his vision of identity and what it means to be African. Both as a Gorée islander and as a proud member of the Mandinka ethnic group, Keita's later paintings turned from the blues and greens of the ocean to the yellows and browns of his native Sahel.

One day, some years later, he appeared at my home with a dramatic abstract acrylic that he offered me in thanks for all my encouragement during his early years. It was called "Khoudia et ses Bijoux" (Khoudia and her Jewels) and had been painted in 1967, the year that we met. It measured 1m50 square and still dominates my living room today, as do several other water colors and engravings by Souleye that I purchased over the years.

He chose to live in New York from 1979 to 1985 and began a long career as an international artist. He became in his turn a professor of ceramic and painting at the Jamaïca Arts Center in New York and showed his work at several prestigious New York galleries. Back in Senegal, he became a board member of Gorée Institute and the Scientific Council of the Biennial event of Dakar.

Dakar-based *Senegalese cultural journalist,* Aboubacar Demba Cissokho who has worked as a reporter for the Senegalese Press Agency (APS) since 2001 wrote:

…On 31 January 2012, at the solemn reception of Arts and Letters, Souleymane Keita was awarded the Grand Prize for the Arts from the President of the Republic of Senegal for his life's work. "He was the only artist to be chosen by the judges unanimously," remarked Alioune Badiane, the chief judge for the arts, on the occasion.

That was well-deserved recognition for an artist of whom the broader public was largely unaware because he had chosen to live unobtrusively, quietly scrutinizing the tumult of his society and his era in his old age. But in the artistic community, the man enjoyed the immense respect that befitted his inborn talent and his ability to translate his aesthetics into a variety of media and to embody the values of spiritual humanism that he shared with his "master of thought," Léopold Sédar Senghor…

We were all profoundly shocked and saddened to learn of Souleye's unexpected death on July 19, 2014 at the age of 67. The Senegalese press reflected the national sense of loss when they wrote:

A Brilliant Creative Spirit Leaves His Mark

The Senegalese painter, Souleymane Keita, died on 19 July at the age of 67 leaving a legacy as a creative spirit overflowing with talent whose modesty was paired with a gift for depicting a unique vision of the universe.

Souleymane Keita 1947-2014

Today, the works of our friend and brother, Souleymane Keita, embellish numerous museums, institutions, presidencies and embassies worldwide.

In 1967, the same year I met El Hadji, Bouna and Souleye Keita, we all watched as the trainers of Senegal's national soccer team (Lamine Diack, Mawade Wade and Joe Diop) were faced with a major challenge in preparing the qualification match for the 1968 African Cup of Nations in Ethiopia. They had to get past the powerful Guinean team made up of such famous African players such as Camara Morlaye, Chérif Souleymane, and Petit Sory. The Senegalese trainers recruited their best players including Louis Gomis, Louis Camara, Yatma Diop and my brother El Hadj Sarr who had brought me into his family.

I was not much of a sports fan, but because of El Hadji and Pape Seck, I became more and more aware of the world of soccer in Senegal. I was so proud to be close to El Hadji. He was a powerful left winger with a disconcerting style who scored many goals and was known as a playmaker through his vision, technique, ball control, creativity, and passing ability. But in addition to his prowess on the soccer field, according to his teammate Yatma Diop "he was known by his teammates for his pleasant disposition, his friendliness and his generosity."

Against all odds, that Senegalese team beat the Guinean team and qualified to play in the 1968 African Cup of Nations. Unfortunately, El Hadj did not go to the finals in Ethiopia but in 1969 went to France to play for Chaumont to replace his friend Souleymane Camara who left to play for another team. In France, El Hadji played for several teams: Chaumont, Sete and Romans-sur-Isere among others.

El Hadji Sarr on Gorée just before leaving for France in 1969

We were delighted when El Hadji met the love of his life, Martine Bartoli who was born in 1953, nine years his junior. She was a beautiful, gentle auburn haired woman with alabaster skin. They married in 1980. El Hadji and Martine had two daughters, Axelle and Mareme. No father ever had greater love for his daughters. They named Mareme in honor of El Hadji's mother, Maria Sambou. He often referred to his second daughter as Yaay Sambou (Mother Sambou) as is the custom in Senegal when a child is named for an older relative.

Martine tragically suffered from multiple sclerosis, an unpredictable often disabling disease of the central nervous system that disrupts the flow of information within the brain and between the brain and the body. When she and El Hadj came for a visit to Senegal, she was already showing signs of loss of coordination. I was moved by her frustration as the disease began

Martine and El Hadji

to take over her life.

El Hadji stood by her through all her ordeals until her death on March 16, 1996 at the age of 43, after 16 years of marriage. El Hadji transferred all his boundless love for Martine to their two children and devoted the next 20 years of his life to raising them to become two fine, intelligent, independent women. Both are today successful English teachers. Axelle moved to the States. She currently lives in San Diego, California with her husband and two teenage children. Mareme lives with her partner in Lyon. She and her sister remain incredibly close despite the distance that separates them.

Axelle's marriage: Mareme, Axelle, El Hadji

I visited El Hadji in France during his early days there. He made a couple of visits back to Senegal, the first while Martine was still alive and then a second visit several years later. We stayed in touch by mail telephone, e-mail and through family connections. We never stopped referring to each other as "my brother."

In over 47 years of living in France, El Hadji never lost his attachment to his Senegalese family. I was struck by the fact that he gradually adopted a French *midi* accent but I realized it was not pretension, but the effects of the environment. He also developed a taste for good French red wine. But whatever changes he underwent living in another culture, his love of Senegal and things Senegalese never diminished. Over the years, El Hadji was instrumental in helping to bring family members to live, study and work in France. Most recently, he arranged a marriage between his sister, Diaw Sarr's older daughter, Madeleine, to a Guinean widower living in France.

Over the years, El Hadji had several major bouts with illness, but generally remained active and in good health. He loved working with young boys and girls in soccer camps. He had dreamed of one day resettling in Senegal an opening a soccer school. But this was never to be. In 2013, he began to fall seriously ill and gradually became unable to continue his activities.

Though we knew El Hadji had been ill, it was only when we read the description by his daughter Mareme of the last three very painful years of her father's life that we came to understand what he had been through prior to his last two weeks in Senegal:

"*...My father fell ill at the end of 2013. In fact, it took the French doctors several months to diagnose his cancer and he had gone through numerous procedures before they announced to him that he had stage four lung cancer. From the beginning they explained to him that the cancer was inoperable and that he would have to undergo a protocol of chemotherapy.*

From there, events unfolded very rapidly. The doctors had to amputate his right leg above the knee because the state of his veins and arteries had deteriorated severely. The pain was unbearable and he was hospitalized for several months. I remember seeing him cry and call out to his dead mother. I was there seated next to him holding his hand and trying to give him support even though deep inside me my whole being was suffering to see the father I adored cry. I think that was the most difficult time I lived through during this long illness. I felt so powerless.

They finally amputated his leg after which he spent several months in a center for amputees in Lyon for a re-education program. While he was at this center, he showed enormous strength of character and an unflappable will. He never complained and inspired the admiration of the health personnel at the center by making rapid progress. The only thing on his mind was to get used to his new prosthetic leg so that he could walk again and go home.

This was the time when I felt the greatest pride at being his daughter. I told myself that my sister, my mother and myself had been extraordinarily lucky to have had this man in our lives. He was simply an exceptional force of love and sacrifice because throughout his many challenges, he was the one who supported us. He kept his sense of humor, was never depressed or at least never showed it, and made sure that we would never worry. I remember the many times he said to me, and I am sure he said it to my sister Axelle as well, "Don't worry about me, I'm alright."

Also, he often repeated that Martine (my mother) had suffered courageously, and for her sake, he did not have the right to complain. As I write these words, I cannot but realize that Axelle and I had extraordinary parents.

At the same time, he was undergoing various chemotherapy treatments that the doctors had to adjust periodically according to the result of the latest scans. His oncologist admired his combativeness and his resistance even though the secondary effects of the chemotherapy had begun to appear. First and foremost was nausea and loss of appetite. This was most worrying for him because he wanted to eat the dishes he liked, but as soon as the plate was presented to him, he was no longer hungry.

This was the beginning of the challenge of nourishing himself as the episodes of nausea came and went in irregular rhythms. I called everyday when we were not together, even if it was only to talk for two minutes, hear his voice, and make my presence felt. It was our little daily ritual. I know he waited assiduously for my calls. I also came to the hospital to visit him during his chemotherapy sessions because he was treated and monitored in Lyon. From time to time, I would bring him home to spend the weekend with us in Lyon.

All this continued until last summer (June-July 2016). He was now coming to Lyon almost every week for radiation therapy because the metastases had migrated to his shoulder and the base of his spine. It was at that time that we had an appointment to discuss his status with his oncologist and it was at that moment that she told him that it no longer made sense to restart chemotherapy treatments because the illness was too advanced. Furthermore, my father was sick of the side effects and wanted to stop the treatments. He obviously asked for my advice and I told him that I did not want to see him suffer and that whatever he decided my sister Axelle and I would stand beside him.

He spoke many times to me and Axelle about wanting to return to Senegal. I asked the doctor for her opinion. She said it was feasible and, if that was his choice, he had to do it so that he would have no regrets. She added: "This trip has to happen as soon as possible. October will be a little too late." Looking back, I now understand that she was saying he would no longer be with us in October, but at the time, I did not fully understand..."

Over those last few years, El Hadji and I spoke frequently by telephone. He often called Senegal to see how I was doing because he heard that I had been ill! There was not a conversation where he did not express his hope, wish, his intention to come back to Senegal for a visit. I was skeptical but humored him in the hopes of raising his spirits. But I had forgotten the determination of that Gorée team left wing attacker I had known years before. Neither time nor disease had weakened his resolve.

It was when I received an e-mail in Dakar from Axelle in July 2016 advising me that they had made a decision concerning an eventual trip by El Hadji to Senegal that I recognized the iron will of my brother El Hadji Sarr:

"...Mareme & I are trying to speed up my Dad's trip to Dakar. He is waiting for mid September to October & has confirmed that his Doctors have given him the green light- he will have to space out his treatments. I am reaching out to see if we can maybe put a little pressure for him to leave France even sooner (early September is ideal)."

And then in early September:

*"...I wanted to let you know the planned trip as it is approaching very soon- given my Dad's current condition, his med team said that he must leave **very soon**- Mareme will forward me the full travel itinerary which I will share with you- she is cced on this email-*

Dates are 9/12-9/26. His Doctor will have meds & prescription ready just in case. He wants to surprise everyone and asked me to tell you to keep the trip a secret (until he gets there)!

As for his daily routine, he may need help bathing - he is in a wheelchair & has a prosthetic leg- he sleeps and rests a lot, so visits will have to be limited and managed. He has lost his appetite and only drinks/eats soup as of now (enriched with vegetables and beef broth for nutrients)

This is his wish and his med team has given us the green light. We know he will be in good hands and only wish we could share his joy & peace when he is back at home...."

I was worried about being able to handle the responsibility of caring for a very sick person since I was not in the best of health, but at the same time was pleased that I would be seeing El Hadji again. I need not have worried, because the whole family mobilized to care for El Hadji while he was in my home, and I became a sort of manager/supervisor.

I began by reorganizing the house for his arrival trying to ensure wheelchair access to key locations, and planning menus that might allow him to eat. I could not maintain the confidentiality he had requested because I had to share the information with my household staff in order to prepare for "a guest in a wheel chair." His niece Maimouna, one of Diaw Sarr's daughters who works for me, quickly figured out what was happening. We soon spread the news to the immediate family that El Hadji was coming.

I tried to imagine what our interactions would be like, but had not counted on how diminished he would be by his illness and how difficult communication had become. In travelling to Senegal, Air France policy required that he wear rather than carry his prosthetic leg. Unfortunately, he had lost so much weight that the leg no longer fit properly on his stump. On arrival in Dakar, the Air France crew insisted that he wear his leg before he deplaned. There followed a humiliating process where he was obliged to take his pants off. By the time he arrived at my house, he was both exhausted and furious at the treatment he had received on the plane. This anger was short lived in the face of his delight at being "home" and seeing members of his family again. Several women from the family turned away to hide their tears at the sight of their emaciated brother/uncle.

By some wonderful coincidence, a dear friend and colleague, Burkinabe public health doctor, Dr. Georges Tiendrebéogo was passing thorough Dakar on a consultation with UNICEF. He usually stayed with me when he came through Dakar and this time, by some miracle, his visit coincided with El Hadji's arrival. "Dr. Georges" as he is known, was invaluable in helping us to care for El Hadji while he was here. He had a medical doctor's perception of what was going on and a bedside manner for dealing with terminal patients that really helped improve not only the quality of El Hadji's life, but the spirits of all of us who were attempting to provide appropriate care as well.

Our younger brother Ousmane died of pancreatic cancer in the US. He had gone to America and married an American woman and had a son. On a visit to Senegal, he fell ill, and on the advice of our brother Dr. Bouna, he returned to the US where he was diagnosed with pancreatic cancer and died after several months. Our older sister, Diaw Sarr never got over the fact that she was absent when her little brother Ousmane died.

Her daughters understood her anguish when El Hadji fell ill and organized a one-month trip for Diaw Sarr to France. She visited her children and grand children living in France and got to spend some time with El Hadji in the town of Romans where he lived. Although she never said it, she knew he was dying and desperately wanted to see him again.

During El Hadji's last two weeks in Dakar, she commuted daily from her home in Yeumbeul on the periphery of Dakar to care for him and manage the flood of family and friends who came to see him. She would go home late in the afternoon and return early the next morning. Two of her daughters who worked for me were also present to ensure the hospitality, errands, cooking and cleaning for all the visitors. Paul Coly slept on the couch next to the spare room where El Hadji was sleeping and got up several times a night to respond to his needs. Dr. Bouna came by daily and coordinated El Hadji's care and support with Dr. Georges.

Despite his emaciated appearance, he floated for the first several days on a sea of familial love and the affection of old friends. The challenge was preparing food he could eat. Initially, he would eat a little, but it gradually became more and more difficult. We all shared a sense of utter helplessness on days when he literally ate nothing at all. A few spoons of soup or a few sips of Sprite became reasons for celebration. At times when Mareme or Axelle called, he was sometimes too weak to speak to them.

As we moved into the second week, it became more and more evident that El Hadji would not be able to travel as an airplane passenger on the 26th of September as scheduled. We began to look into possibilities for medical evacuation, or moving him to a clinic where he could be fed by drips, made more comfortable and perhaps brought back to a state where he could travel.

On the morning of the 26th of September when El Hadji was supposed to fly back to France, Dr. Georges came into my bedroom, which was very unusual because out of respect, people do not usually come into my bedroom when I am sleeping. I am a nocturnal being and since my retirement I tend to go to sleep very late and get up late in the morning. But on that day at around 6:30 a.m., George gently woke me from a restless sleep, took a few minutes to greet me and allow me to wake up, and calmly informed me that El Hadji had passed away in the guest room at around 5 a.m. that same morning.

In the Moslem religion, people have to be buried within 24 hours of their death, preferably the same day before the setting of the sun. The family communication processes went into high gear to inform everyone in Dakar, France and the US that El Hadji had passed away. The women of the family arrived in tears that morning and took their turns viewing his body in the guest room and saying goodbye to his mortal remains. At a moment when I was alone with his remains, I took his cold hand in mine and whispered to my now peaceful brother: "*Au revoir mon frère, Sarr, Sarr gelem...*"

The men of the family mobilized, some contacting the imam of the local mosque, others going out to get the required death and inhumation certificates, arrange for a hearse and small buses to transfer mourners, prepare radio and press obituaries and move the cadaver to the morgue room at the mosque where several family members purchased the necessary percale, perfume, cotton and incense to prepare the body. By 5 p.m., prayers were being said before his cadaver at the mosque and he was transported to the local cemetery where El Hadji Sarr was buried next to his father, Pa Bouna Souleymane Sarr.

At 5:45 p.m., I found myself sitting in a row of chairs in front of my house next to my older sister, Diaw Sarr, along with other close family members to receive the condolences of the hundreds of mourners who returned from the burial or passed by the house. That day, many of the same people I had met over 45 years ago on my first trips to the island of Gorée filed by the seated family members. The departed Pape Seck, Souleymane Keita, our brother Ousmane and several other friends who had already passed away were sorely missed, for they surely would have been there to say goodbye were they still alive. The imam and a couple of family members made short speeches. Each visitor received a small sachet of candy and biscuits and, as night began to fall, the mourners began to disperse slowly.

A couple of days after the burial, El Hadji's daughters Axelle and Mareme arrived from San Diego and Lyon as did nephew, Diaw Sarr's son, Papisse Gadio, a gourmet chef from Marseille. They all visited the cemetery and participated in the ceremonies and gatherings following the burial before returning home. Diaw Sarr, together with the other members of the family, all acting as one very efficient entity, took over planning, shopping and cooking for the third day and eighth day gatherings of hundreds of family and friends at the family home in the suburb of Yeumbeul.

Axelle, Mareme and Papisse stayed at my house and we were able to spend time together consoling each other, sharing meals and memories, getting to know each other better and learning about things that had happened in each of our lives that we had missed. We reflected on how international the next generation of the Sarr family was. From the core Senegalese family, the children and grandchildren have developed alliances and connections with France, USA, Algeria, Mexico, Madagascar, Mali, Guinea, Burkina Faso. For Axelle and Mareme, their time together with the family was certainly cathartic and helped them better to understand how much their father had been loved as well as the immense network they were part of.

*In the obituary in the newspaper of the Haute-Marne (**Haute-Marne** is a department in the northeast of France) of September 29, 2017, homage was paid to the memory of El Hadji Sarr.*

EL HADJI SARR IS NO MORE

El Hadji Sarr arrived at Chaumont (France) in June 1969 to play soccer. He arrived from Senegal where he was born on November 3, 1944 in Dakar to replace his friend Souleymane Camara who left to play for another team.

El Hadji Sarr was a powerful left winger with a disconcerting style who scored many goals.

He played in Second Division Pro with ECAC for four seasons before transferring to the Sète football club. Towards the end of his career he played for several clubs in the South-East of France before settling on Romans-sur-Isère. That is where he founded his family. He frequently visited Chaumont to see his many friends and former soccer players.

El Hadji Sarr, who suffered for many years from a long illness, expressed his wish to spend two weeks in Dakar. Unfortunately, he was unable to complete his stay. He passed away in the city of his birth on September 26.

The sporting world of Haute Marne will remember him as a brilliant player of exceptional kindness. The Journal of the Haute Marne extends its condolences to his family.

AFTERWORD:
MAREME SARR

" I feel lost, and I have to admit that my father was my reference point and my safe place in this world. He never judged my sister or myself and always supported us. He had boundless love for his family and I know that Axelle and I were the center of his world, of his universe. All his decisions were made to protect us and to nourish us in our lives. I don't think I ever witnessed stronger paternal love. He was so proud of us...

Axelle, Mareme and El Hadji

What frightens me the most at the moment is that time is erasing my pain and little by little his memory is fading. I don't want that to happen. I want to remember constantly that I suffer from his absence. I want the whole world to pay tribute to him and want people to know that El Hadji Sarr existed on this earth and that he was wonderful and exceptional, that he loved my mother to the end despite the challenges of her illness, and that he loved both his daughters unconditionally."

REFLECTIONS

◇◇◇

Through the intervention of El Hadji Sarr, I had had the privilege of being introduced into an extraordinary Senegalese family. And I say extraordinary because it was only as time went by and I got to know other families more intimately that I realized that not all families were as welcoming or had the peace and harmony I found in the Sarr compound. In many families you find conflict between co-wives and the children of co-wives, between brothers and sisters fighting over inheritance, between Moslems and Catholics in the same family. You find people who have sacrificed all their human values for material gain and see the other as nothing more than an opportunity for making a profit. It took me some time to get over my naiveté in thinking that the Sarr family was typical. They were not. They set the bar high for the quality of human relations and many other families paled in comparison. El Hadji

El Hadji Sarr 1944–2016

was a product of this wonderful family and consequently, as his daughter Mareme said, "…he was wonderful, he was exceptional," and much more.

That day, sitting in front of my house, receiving condolences, I was no longer on the outside looking in. I was one of the bereaved, one of the mourners. An African proverb says that "No matter how long a bamboo stick stays in the river it never becomes a crocodile" but that day I was not feeling my difference. I realized that the Jewish boy from Brooklyn had come a long way speaking French and Wolof and appreciating Senegalese culture first hand and being able to see the values that underpinned people's actions and explained what they did and why they did it. And I was an accepted, functioning member of a Senegalese family, a precious relationship that has lasted for over forty-five years. The Senegalese say: *Luu duul degg, du yagg*" (What is not true does not last.) But then the opposite must also apply: "What is true, lasts for a long time."